GREEK WITHOUT TEARS

GREEK
WITHOUT TEARS

A Basic Study of the New Testament Language

TED EDWARDS

Edited by
D. V. PALMER

Foreword by
CLINTON CHISHOLM

RESOURCE *Publications* • Eugene, Oregon

GREEK WITHOUT TEARS
A Basic Study of the New Testament Language

Copyright © 2014 Ted Edwards. All rights reserved. Except for brief quotations in critical publications or reviews, no part of this book may be reproduced in any manner without prior written permission from the publisher. Write: Permissions. Wipf and Stock Publishers, 199 W. 8th Ave., Suite 3, Eugene, OR 97401.

Resource Publications
An Imprint of Wipf and Stock Publishers
199 W. 8th Ave., Suite 3
Eugene, OR 97401

www.wipfandstock.com

ISBN 13: 978-1-62564-098-7

Manufactured in the U.S.A.   06/19/2014

Some Scripture quotations are from the HOLY BIBLE, NEW INTERNATIONAL VERSION; copyright © 1973, 1978, 1984, 2010 by the International Bible Society, and Biblica, Inc.™ Used by permission. All rights reserved worldwide.

Other Scripture quotations are from the *Di Jamiekan Nyuu Testiment* Kingston: Bible Society of the West Indies, 2012.

Scripture quotations identified as NRSV are from the New Revised Standard Version of the Bible, copyright 1989 by the Division of Christian Education of the National Council of Churches of Christ in the U.S.A. Used by permission. All rights reserved.

All quotations marked NET are taken from the NETBible® copyright ©1996–2006 by Biblical Studies Press, L.L.C. www.bible.org All rights reserved.

Scripture quotations identified REB are from The Revised English Bible published jointly by the Oxford University Press and Cambridge University Press, 1989. All rights reserved.

BWHEBB, BWHEBL, BWTRANSH [Hebrew]; BWGRKL, BWGRKN, and BWGRKI[Greek] Postscript® Type 1 and TrueTypeTfonts Copyright © 1994–2009 BibleWorks, LLC. All rights reserved. These Biblical Greek and Hebrew fonts are used with permission and are from BibleWorks, software for Biblical exegesis and research.

CONTENTS

Foreword by Clinton Chisholm | ix
Acknowledgments | xi
Acknowledgments (2014) | xiii
Introduction To Grammar | xv
Abbreviations | xxiii

Chapter 1
The Greek Alphabet | 1

Chapter 2
Recognizing and Increasing Your Greek Vocabulary | 4

Chapter 3
Greek—*Babel* or Science of Sound Changes? | 8

Chapter 4
Greek Present Tense | 15

Chapter 5
Greek—Circumstances Alter Cases | 19

Chapter 6
Greek Prefixes and Infixes as Time Determinants | 23

Chapter 7
Prefixes | 27

Chapter 8
Agreement or Concord | 30

Chapter 9
Every Speech Sound has a Meaning | 34

Chapter 10
Participles and Their Uses | 36

Chapter 11
The Subjunctive Mood | 39

Chapter 12
Having Fun with Numbers and the Infinitive Mood as well | 41

Chapter 13
Vowel Contractions—Crasis | 45

Chapter 14
Conditional Clauses | 48

Chapter 15
Third Declension | 50

Chapter 16
Optative Mood & Vocabulary Aids | 52

Chapter 17
Oh Mi, Oh Mai | 56

Chapter 18 | 59

Chapter 19
Review—Differences in Expressing Greek and English | 61

APPENDICES

Appendix A | 65

Appendix B
Irregular Verb Forms Found in John Chapter 1 and Their Derivatives | 69

Appendix C
Table of the Regular Verb | 71

EXCURSUS

Excursus A
A Syntactic-Analytic New Testament Greek Study
with a New Pedagogical Consideration | 77

Excursus B
John 1:1–18: Block Diagramming of JNT, NIV, GNT | 95

Excursus Γ
The Language of the New Testament | 107

Excursus Δ
15 Reasons why Jamaican Patois is a Language? | 112

Greek-English Vocabulary | 115
Helpful Material | 133

FOREWORD

The aim of this booklet is to encourage the study of Greek by English and Jamaican speaking peoples, who have been singularly blessed by a rich heritage of words, which have come to them directly from the Greek, or through various other languages. There are so many of these words that at one time I thought that there was no English language. I now think it is one of the most enriched languages. Enriched with borrowing from many sources: from Sanskrit, Latin and other tongues. Greek, however, has played a larger part than is realized.

This booklet will also apply for the first time, as far as I know, a theory expressed by the Apostle Paul in 1 Cor 14:10 that every speech sound has a significance. The greater accuracy that can be obtained by this system is illustrated by the Greek word *Kalos*. This word originally 'ikalos' is made up of three speech sounds: "ik' which means 'fit or suitable,' 'al' which is 'equal to all' and 'os' which tells the number, gender and case of the noun described.

The literal meaning so obtained is 'all fit.' When you check a good Greek Lexicon, you will find many beautiful synonyms as: beautiful, good, fertile, rich, worthy, proper, which all fit in well in some contexts. For example: Paul in 1 Cor. 7:1 says: It is good for a man not to be attached to a woman. Here the word 'good' is describing an all fit principle. Obviously 'fit and proper' would be more enlightening than 'good,' since Paul was not advocating the virtues of non attachment. In colloquial English we would say, "It

Foreword

is okay." You will find however, that the synonyms do not always fit into every context, but the literal meaning is always suitable. This will be a good way of checking to see if you have come upon the exact meaning.

Again this system not only gains in accuracy, but it provides a means of increasing your vocabulary rapidly, since the relationship to English is in most cases more easily seen in the syllables than in the whole word.

Another advantage of this system is that the oneness of all languages will be more clearly seen, and that mankind will one day again speak one language, and so re-label the Babel. I believe this will happen when He comes. Till then, let us have some exciting fun exploring the Greek language.

Clinton Chisholm

ACKNOWLEDGMENTS

Greek Without Tears has been made possible by the contribution of so many persons and books that it will take another book to enumerate.

Special thanks, however, must be made to the following: the late J. J. Mills former Vice-Principal of Mico College who showed in his lectures that learning could be fun.

To H. F. Edwards, my brother and former tutor, who first brought to my attention the similarities between German and English.

To Lancelot Ogden, who in his book *Loom of Language* made available the discoveries of 'Grimm and Rask' concerning the inter-relationship of languages.

To H. F. Hudson who in his book *Teach Yourself New Testament Greek*, showed that by divesting the texts of unnecessary accents, there need not be any bullying to learn the common language of Alexander the Great.

To Ernest Cadman Colwell and Ernest W. Tune who in their *A Beginner's Reader: Grammar for New Testament Greek*, limited their aims to developing the ability to read New Testament Greek, thus freeing the learner from the drudgery of much translating from English to Greek.

To the men who distinguished between things that differ: Richard C. Trench in *Synonyms of the New Testament*. A. T. Robertson in *Grammar of the Greek New Testament in the Light of*

Acknowledgments

Historical Research and his *New Short Grammar of the Greek Testament*; W. E. Vine's *Expository Dictionary of New Testament* Words; F. Blass and A. Debrunner, *A Greek Grammar of the New Testament and Other Early Christian Literature* translated by Robert W. Funk.

H. P. V. Nunn's *Elements of New Testament Greek* as well as J. W. Wenham's *Revision* for the idea of an introductory review in basic English grammar.

To Ray Summer's *Essentials of New Testament Greek* for emphasising eight cases instead of five.

To all who loaned me books—Mr. Rex Major, MTh, of the Bahamas, Rev. Phillip Price, MA, retired Archdeacon of Cornwall, Jamaica.

To the Saint James Parish Library whose books on Linguistics were invaluable.

To all those who encouraged me to greater and greater accuracy: Professor F. F. Bruce, Mr. H. L. Clacken and my patient, understanding wife, Deloris, who was usually the first to share my deepening insight of the Word of God, even as she prepared my breakfast.

Special thanks is due to Miss Hyacinth Urquhart, who painstakingly typed the original manuscripts, writing the Greek letters where this was necessary, to Miss C. Bola, who helped in typing the final manuscripts and to Mr. Anthony 'Tony' Norman, BA (Hons.), for designing the cover.

To God Be the Glory!

ACKNOWLEDGMENTS (2014)

Special thanks to Dr Bradley Edwards and Mrs Yissi Edwards-Geddes (children of the author) for their encouragement in giving their father's Greek grammar a new lease on life. Thanks also to Brianna Manley, NYU undergrad, for her expert typing of the manuscript, Yissi and Joy Richards for being a part of the revision team, and to the editorial committee of *CJET* for permission to edit and employ material for Excursus a.

D. V. Palmer

INTRODUCTION TO GRAMMAR

Since not everyone who wants to study Greek has had formal acquaintance with the Grammar of Languages of the Greek family, it is essential that certain grammatical terms be introduced at the beginning. At the risk of boring those who already know these, let us look at the more important of these.

PARTS OF SPEECH

The role played by a word in a sentence determines its part of speech.

Since some words are capable of performing various roles, their parts of speech can only be known when they are in a sentence e.g., (a) <u>Fire</u> the oven. (b) Kindle the <u>fire</u>. (c) A <u>fire</u>fly. In (a) it is a verb. In (b) it is a noun. In (c) it is an adjective.

Words are therefore classified according to their roles as follows:

1. NOUNS—names of persons, places and things. Things include quality e.g., beauty; feeling e.g., hatred; persons e.g., Peter; places e.g., Galilee; things e.g., book, feast.
2. ADJECTIVES—which describe nouns by expressing their qualities: *beautiful* grass; *clear* sky.
3. PRONOUNS—which point to a person, place or thing without naming it: *I, you.*

Introduction To Grammar

4. VERBS—which tell an action or state: The man *runs*. The girl *sits*.

5. ADVERBS—which modify and limit verbs, adjectives and other adverbs: The sun shone *brightly*. The walls were *slightly* grey.

6. PREPOSITIONS—which show in what relation one thing stands to another thing: He walked *through* the streets. His hand was *under* the table.

7. CONJUNCTIONS—which connect words, phrases, clauses and sentences: He went into the shop *that* he might buy bread *and* sugar. N.B. *that* connects two clauses, *and* connects two nouns.

8. INTERJECTIONS—words of exclamation: Alas! Behold!

The ARTICLE is sometimes classed as a separate part of speech, but it is, in fact, a demonstrative adjective. They are two kinds: Definite viz. *the* and Indefinite viz. *a, an*.

The is the equivalent to *this* or *that* and is found in the Greek.

A, an are not found and their significance must be determined from the context.

Determine the Parts of Speech of the words underlined in the following sentence:

I *never saw* such a thing *before*, that the beggar *who* was standing *before* the gate, should take *the* book *before he* had paid *for* it.

To gain facility in spotting the parts of speech used in a sentence, try practising with some sentences that you meet in reading.

Introduction To Grammar

Kinds of Nouns

There are four kinds:

- Names of Persons and Places   Proper
  e.g., Paul, Ephesus
- Names applicable to many in a group   Common
  e.g., boy, tree
- Name of a group taken together   Collective
  e.g., committee, jury
- Names describing qualities or state   Abstract
  e.g., goodness

In many languages Nouns have triangular references, that is, they differ in three ways: Number, Gender and Case.

In Greek as in English there are 2 Numbers: Singular referring to one thing, and Plural, referring to more than one thing.

There are three Genders in English: masculine, feminine and neuter. In English these respectively refer to the male sex, the female sex and things of neither sex.

In Greek these Genders do not necessarily tell the sex or lack of it. For example, a child is considered neuter in Greek.

Cases are most important in Greek. At this stage we can merely introduce you to the various cases and their significance. Let us take the sentence: "O John, give Mary's book to Tom at the desk."

John is here addressed. Because we are calling to John, we say that John is in the Vocative case.

Book tells us what must be given and is in the accusative case.

Mary's tells us of whom or from whom the book came. In Greek of Mary is Genitive, from Mary is Ablative. The distinction would be seen in the context.

To Tom is dative. In the Greek, the dative case is used to translate "to or for a thing" (true Dative); as well as "by or with a thing,"

Introduction To Grammar

Instrumental Case; as well as the location of a thing called the Locative Case. Thus at the desk would be placed in the Locative Case.

THE CASES ARE:

- NOMINATIVE - Subject e.g., The BOY jumps. Boy is nominative
- VOCATIVE - Person addressed. i.e. it tells Who is addressed
- ACCUSATIVE - Object e.g., I heeded the voice. Voice tells what is heeded.
- GENITIVE - Of a thing, or person e.g., Mary's
- ABLATIVE - From a thing e.g., from the voice
- DATIVE - To or for a thing or person
- LOCATIVE - At a place
- INSTRUMENTAL - By or with a person or thing.

Luckily only 5 of these forms you will have to learn since the Genitive and Ablative are identical, while the Dative, Locative and Instrumental are the same in Greek.

Adjectives

These must agree with the nouns they qualify in NUMBER, GENDER, AND CASE.

Verbs

Verbs are distinguishable in 5 ways: Number, Person, Voice, Mood and Tense.

Introduction To Grammar

Number and Person : The person tells who is speaking—1st person e.g., I, we; who is spoken to—2nd Person e.g., thou, you, or who is spoken of—3rd Person e.g., they, he, she, it, Tom, Jews.

Since personal pronouns are not used by themselves except for emphasis, personal endings are attached to the stem to distinguish both the person and the number of the verb e.g., The Greek Letter ω is added to the stem λυ = loose to form λυω = I loose

εις is added to λυ to form λυεις = you loose (singular)

ει is added to λυ to form λυει = he, she, it looses

ομεν is added to λυ to form λυομεν = we loose

ετε is added to lu to form λυετε = you loose (plural; *unu* [Jamaican])

ουσι is added to λυ to form λυουσι they loose.

You have now been introduced to ω which resembles the English W, but which is really a double o or large O, hence its Greek name Omega. Greek *mega* = great.

Note also the strange l = l and the two forms of 's.' One looks like a cursive s turned the wrong way and the other almost like the printed ς.

Note, too, that what looks like a 'v' is really a Greek *n*. What they would have christened NIK we would have christened VIK. History tells us of such a battering ram used in a war by the name of NIK.

Learn carefully the above endings, they tell us not only the Person but the Number of the Persons involved with the verb.

VOICES

There are three grammatical Voices illustrated by the following sentences.

ACTIVE: The dog bit the boy. Here the subject "dog" is the active participant.

PASSIVE: The boy was bitten by the dog. Here the subject "boy" is the passive recipient of the action.

But look at this, Mary marries Tom. Here, both were active, and both were passive. The Greek answer to this would be to use the MIDDLE Voice. English has no middle voice.

There is a class of verbs which are Passive in form but Active in meaning. These are called Deponents because they have put away their Active form. These words are usually reflexive or intransitive, i.e. they do not take an object e.g., He is striving.

Moods are divided into two classes (a) Assertive i.e. those that make a statement or ask a question or fact—Indicative Mood e.g., He is here. Are you coming? and those that give command Imperative Mood—e.g., Go.

(b) Non Assertive—Here wishful thinking predominates, and matters are advanced for the sake of argument e.g., If I give my body to be burned, I would not be happy. This is the subjunctive Mood which is supposing something for the sake of argument.

Unfulfilled wishes also fall in this class and are called Optative Moods e.g., Would that she were here. In fact, she was not there but the wish is to have it otherwise.

Tense in English shows principally time: Present, Past or Future. Greek however, introduces a durative element telling whether the action is continuous and can be represented by a line _____. or punctiluous and can be represent by a dot . The aorist may show completed action e.g., He wrote. NB. He is no longer writing.

The Aorist Tense is the tense used in the Greek sometime to show action at a fixed time (hour) while the Present (e.g., I am singing) and the Imperfect (e.g., I was singing) are used to show continuous or linear action.[1]

Phrases

A phrase is a group of words in which no finite verb is either expressed or understood. e.g., To forgive the man in the street is easy. 'To forgive' is a noun phrase since it is the subject of the sentence. 'In the street' is an adjectival phrase since it qualifies man.

Clauses

Clauses and phrases are classified according to their function in the sentence; e.g., He sat on the table. 'On the table' is a phrase telling where he sat. This is therefore an adverb phrase.

Example 2: He was the man *that stole the cat*. 'That stole the cat' is an adjective clause since it qualifies 'man.'

Adverb or adverbial Clauses are further divided into eight classes as follows:

1. Final—This denotes purpose. For example,
2. he was sent *that (in order that) he might tell*
3. Temporal—This denotes time. For example,
4. *when he had finished he left.*
5. Local—This denotes place. For example, He went *where the daisies grew.*
6. Causal—This denotes cause. For example, He left *because he was angry.*

---

[1]. Those who are not acquainted with Jamaican should know that the verb "to be" is sometimes omitted in the Greek, e.g., "Good to walk in righteousness" is best rendered, "It is good to walk in righteousness."

Introduction To Grammar

7. Consecutive—This shows consequence or result. For example, He was so tall *that he could not enter* the room.

8. Conditional—This tells the condition. For example, *If anyone believes in me*, he shall not perish.

9. Concessive—This concedes something; that is, it allows that something may be so. For example, *Although he may be poor*, yet he is honest.

10. Comparative—This is used to compare. For example, He is taller *than John* (is tall).

NOTE: The clauses are italicized.

ABBREVIATIONS

BAG	Bauer, W., et al., eds. *A Greek-English Lexicon of the New Testament and Other Early Christian Literature*. Revised by F. W. Danker. Chicago: Chicago University Press, 1957.
BDF	Blass, F., A. Debrunner, and R. Funk. *A Greek Grammar of the New Testament and Other Early Christian Literature*. Chicago: University Press, 1961.
BT	*Bible Translator*
cf.	*confer*, compare
CGST	Caribbean Graduate School of Theology
CJET	*Caribbean Journal of Evangelical Theology*
CJRS	*Caribbean Journal of Religious Studies*
DM	Dana and Mantey
EGT	*The Expositor's Greek Testament*
et al.	*et alii*, and others
GELS	*Greek-English Lexicon of the Septuagint*
GTJ	*Grace Theological Journal*
GK	Greek
Ibid	*ibidem*, in the same place
IVP	Intervarsity Press

Abbreviations

JNT	*Di Jamiekan Nyuu Testiment* Kingston: Bible Society of the West Indies, 2012
KJV	King James Version
LNJ.	P. Louw, and Eugene A. Nida, eds. *Greek-English Lexicon of the New Testament Based on Semantic Domains*. New York: United Bible Societies, 1988
LXX	Septuagint
MMJ.	H Moulton and George Milligan. *The Vocabulary of the Greek Testament*. Grand Rapids: Eerdmans, 1930
NET	New English Translation (NETBible)
NIV	New International Version
NLT	New Living Translation
NRSV	New Revised Standard Version
NT	New Testament
Op. cit.	*opere citato*, work cited
OT	Old Testament
UBS	United Bible Societies
UBS4	Aland, Barbara, and Kurt Aland, Johannes Karavidopoulos, Carlo M. Martini, Bruce Metzger, K Elliger, W. Rudolph, eds. *Biblia Sacra Utriusque Testamenti Editio Hebraica et Graeca*. Stuttgart: Deutsche Bibelgesellshaft, 1994.
UPA	University Press of America
Vol.	Volume

Chapter 1

THE GREEK ALPHABET

As you begin the study of the Greek language, you will require a Greek dictionary. Such a lexicon is placed at the back or some copies of The Greek New Testament published by the United Bible Societies.

The first two letters Alpha and Beta, when combined, give the origin of the word Alphabet. Look them up. Note their similarities with the English A and B. Observe both capital and common letters. Note also their differences.

Your next letter is Gamma. Note that the capital form is almost a 'C,' but that the common form is almost a 'g.'

Practise writing your ABC or as the Greeks saw it your ABG.

Your next letter as a capital, is shaped like the delta of a river. Its name is Delta—the English D. Note how similar is the common delta to the English d.

Greek without Tears

Next follows your second vowel e. This is called Epsilon. Psilos means bare or simple, and Epsilon represents the uncompounded e. Shortly we will meet another e.

In English the alphabet would next proceed with FGH but Greek no longer uses F since it has a substitute PH. It has already had G combined with C. (Note Spanish Gato and English Cat are referring to the same animal) and H would be confused with another letter. It is therefore shown by a reversed comma ' written over the first letter of vowels and R to show its presence. In place of these three we find the "Zeth" set i.e., Zeta Eta, Theta. This is an upset. Pardon the play on the word upset. For the English Z and its relatives have moved up the ladder. Eta is the second E of the Greek language it is equivalent to Ea or Eh. Hence could be called a compound E or a diphthong. i.e. a double sound.

Next follows Iota which is also Jota because it does the duty of I and J.

Kappa Lambda Mu Nu Represent K, L, M, N, and should be carefully examined for similarities and differences. N.B. common N looks like a V and did help to confuse the languages. e.g., GK NIK = Lat. VIC = to overcome, to gain victory.

Xi is an erratic. It has wandered out of place. This comes before our next vowel Omicron. Greek micro means small. Hence this represents our ordinary English O.

Pi English P comes next and does duty for P and Qu. Since the Greek Quot is no longer used. e.g., GK POU = Latin QUO i.e. where, whither.

Rho, Sigma Tau, Upsilon represent R, S, T, U. Note there are two common forms for S. The more familiar form is used only at the end of a word. Note the resemblance of capital U to Y. This accounts for words as psychology. The first 'y' was a 'u' in the Greek.

Between the vowel u and the last letter the I's have it. We have Phi, Chi and Psi. The three I's. In Jamaica we would probably say the I threes. They are equivalent to Ph, Ch, and Ps pronounced Ph as in Phillip, Ch as in loch and Ps as in psalms. N.B. the forms.

Last but by no means least is Omega. Mega means great. Note the size and shape of the capital Omega and the resemblance of the common Omega to w. It is a compound O = Oa, Oh, otherwise called double O or double u, hence w.

Here follows for easy reference your Greek alphabet, first as capitals then as common letters.

Α Β Γ Δ Ε Ζ Η Θ Ι Κ Λ Μ Ν Ξ Ο Π Ρ Σ Τ Υ Φ Χ Ψ Ω

α β γ δ ε ζ η θ ι κ λ μ ν ξ ο π ρ σ τ υ φ χ ψ ω

In order by name, they are:

Alpha, Beta, Gamma . . . (complete the list)

Chapter 2

RECOGNIZING AND INCREASING YOUR GREEK VOCABULARY

Now that you have learned to recognize the Greek letters and their English equivalents, let us surprise ourselves by the number of Greek words we use in everyday conversation.

Greek Form	English Form
καθαρσις	Catharsis[1]
αρθριτις	arthritis
ασμα	asthma
δυσεντερια	dysentery[2]
φαντασια	phantasia
δογμα	dogma
δραμα	drama

1. Note C for K and final ς in the Greek different from 's' in the word.
2. Note 'U' and final 'ia' of the Greek is usually Y in English.

Recognizing and Increasing Your Greek Vocabulary

ηχω	echo
ιδεα	idea
κριτεριον	criterion
͑οριζων	horizon[3]
βασις	basis
χαρακτηρ	character
πανακεια	panacea[4]
γανγγραινα	gangreina[5] (gangrene)
ἀγγελος	angelos (angel)
παραλυσις	paralysis
͑ρευματισμος	rheumatismos rheumatism[6]
θοραξ	thorax

Beside these Greek words which have resisted change, are many more which have come down to us in compounded forms, e.g., Geography comes from two roots—geo from γη meaning earth, and *graphein* to write. Thus, geography was basically a writing or description of the earth. Here are listed a few:

English	Greek Roots	Meaning of Roots
Basis	βασις	foot
Pedagogue	παιδος αγωγη	child-train
Autonomy	αυτος νομος	self-law or custom

3. Note the rough breathing for the 'h.'
4. Note ει to i or e.
5. Note gg changes to ng.
6. Note rh for ͑ρ.

5

Greek without Tears

Biology	βιος λογος	life—discourse, study or word
Hyperbole	῾υπερ βολη	over-toss, throw
Agnostic	α γνωσις	a—i.e., negative[7]

Orthodoxy	ορθος δοξα	right, straight—opinion
Heterodoxy	῾ετερος δοξα	other, different—opinion
Energy	εν εργον	in—work
Euthanasia	ευ θανατος	well—death
Egocentric	εγω κεντρον	I—centre(ed)
Catalysis	κατα λυσις	down—loosing

There are, too, many English words ending in 'ic' or 'ics.' These comprise a Greek stem plus the Greek 'ikos.' The following is a list with their roots and liberal meanings.

English	Greek Roots	Literal Meaning
Aesthetic	αισθησι ικος	Apt for perception
Dynamic	δυναμις ικος	suitable for power
Therapeutic	θεραπεια ικος	suitable for attending, caring[8]
Comic	κωμος ικος	fit for revel or comedy
Mathematics	μαθημα ικος	things fit for learners, students,
Mimetic	μιμησις ικος	fit for (miming) imitation
Mnemonic	μνησις ικος	suitable for the memory

7. Here + knowledge.
8. Healing.

Recognizing and Increasing Your Greek Vocabulary

Pragmatic	πραγμα ικος	suitable for practice, deeds
Pneumatic	πνευμα ικος	suitable for air, breath or spirit
Acoustic	ακου ικος	suitable for hearing
Phonetics	φωνη ικος	things suitable for sound or voice
Ecclesiastic	εκκλησια ικος	apt, fit or suitable for the church.[9]
Heroic	ηρως ικος	fit for a hero (demi-god)

Note these literal meanings should be checked with a good dictionary for possible changes of usage today.

Explore additional English words with Greek origins. This will not only accelerate your Greek vocabulary study, but your command of English will improve.

To help you to spot some of these, look out for words ending in 'ize,' 'ine,' 'ic,' 'ical,' 'y,' 'is,' 'ia,' 'logy,' 'ism,' 'ea.' Check, too, for words with 'y' in the middle, e.g., physical. Also words beginning with ph, ps, cata, dia, meta, syn, auto, anti, pro, hyper, poly, hypo, epi, peri, z, pn, ch.

Happy Hunting!

Use a dictionary that has the Greek roots from which words originate and compile a list.

Remember every sound has a meaning.

---

[9]. Note, ecclesiastical is pertaining to the Church.

Chapter 3

GREEK—*BABEL* OR SCIENCE OF SOUND CHANGES?

In this chapter we will deal with the evidences of linguistic changes in languages with particular reference to the changes from the Greek language to the English language.

The changes are of two kinds—from Babels and Sound Babels. You will have already noticed the changes in the letters of the alphabet, e.g., capital gamma being written almost like C, i.e. Γ, and common gamma partly as g and partly as y i.e. γ. You must not be surprised to find these letters doing in the English words the duties of the Greek gamma.

For example, as g in γεωργος, this word is made up of two roots γη= earth and εργ= work; thus George is an earth worker. It is not without reason that we hear of farmer George. He has been elevated from cultivator and husbandman to agriculturist and agronomist.

As y in γε = English yea, indeed, notice Greek uses the simple ε to distinguish this from the Greek root meaning earth.

Greek—Babel *or Science of Sound Changes?*

See also αγγελος pronounced *angelos*. This is made up of three parts—an = up, gel = yell, and os which tells the number, case and often the gender of the word. This then means one who yells up, and is variously translated announcer, messenger and angel.

As C, gamma is seldom encountered in the Babel from Greek to English, but is very frequent from Spanish to English, e.g., gato = cat.

English C is usually represented by the Greek K. For example, akou = hearken, from which we get the English 'acoustic.'

Other form Babels worth noting are the Greek Eta, Pi, Rho, Nu and Omega. Their significance has already been dealt with in the study of the alphabet.

Sound Babels are of greater significance in the Greek to English shift than is usually recognised.

As early as 1817 Rasmus Rask, a young Dane, drew attention to sound shifts in the Indo-European group of languages. These were developed and named as Grimm's Law.

Until recent years Grimm's Law was ignored. Men thought that Grimm was better off confining his attention to his fairy tales. The circle below shows the shift as Grimm saw it, if we take them in order around the circle. Or triangle

CONSONANTS BY CLASSES

CLASS	FLAT	SHARP	ASPIRATED	LIQUIDS
LABIALS	B, V, (W)	P	Ph, (Wh)	M
DENTALS/ SIBILANTS	D Z	T S, SS, Ps, Ks	Th Sh	N
GUTTERALS	G	K, Q, Ks	Ch, J	R, L

N.B. Liquid changes are vertical. All other classes are lateral.

Greek without Tears

What Grimm did not point out was that the changes could be classified as (a) Gutteral changes—k, ch, g (b) dental changes—t, th, d and (c) Labial changes—p, f, b. Here then is a law of sound shifts. Sounds have shifted from tongue to tongue on the basis of their classification. (Ted's Law).

The principal classes of consonant sounds are Gutterals, Dentals, Labials, Sibilants, e.g., S, Z, Xi, Psi and Liquids—L, M, N, R.

Sibilants are attracted to the Dentals, e.g., 'the' is pronounced as the, te, de or ze. Another example, of the Sibilant-Dental shift is seen in the Greek ss to tt. For example *glossa* (tongue, language) has come in English in both forms—glossary, diglot. The attic form tt is the form usually passed on to the English, e.g., κρεισσων= greater. Note the gutteral k to g, double ss to English t. Compare German 'strauss' to English "street." (Hebrew 1:4. better = greater).

Liquids M and N are observable changed from Greek to Latin. The shirt from L to R is noted from one kind of Greek to another. Native Chinese pronounce R as L, e.g., "You too cly cly!" meaning *cry cry*; or "You no see fi mi *labbi* pass here?" meaning "Have you seen my rabbit pass here?"

Note Greek κλαι-ω = I cry (Matt. 2:18). cf. Matt. 7:7 κρο-ω= cry. Rev. 3:20

Here are some examples of these sound shifts. Try to pronounce these until you see the connection. Only the roots are mentioned. The changeable parts of the word which show number, gender, case, person, tense, voice and mood are omitted.

GREEK	ENGLISH	KIND OF SHIFTS
φαγειν	FAG, EAT	form shift
εσθ	eat	sibilant + dental s to t andto t = ett. Note English eat. cf. Comestibles

Greek—Babel or Science of Sound Changes?

φερ to f.	bear, ferry	Labial φ to b. Also form shift φ
πατηρ	father	Labial π to f, dental τ to th.
γινω (σκ) k.[1]	know	sk = increasing in. Gutteral to
κειρ	shear	k to ch pronounced at times as sh. Compare:- Charing Cross
χαιρ meanings?	cheer	Did this give 'grace' two
		Something for cheering? Something shared, i.e. a gift.
GK. χαρις		
Φαυλ(ος)	vile	Labial ph for v.
βελτιων	more virtuous	B for V, l for r

These changes, however, must always be checked with a good lexicon because words have been known to change their meanings over a period of time. For example, in 1 Thess. 4:15, the word 'prevent' which originally meant 'to go before' now means 'to hinder.' The older meaning is more relevant as a rule.

Another example is in 1 Corinthians 7:1 where 'touch' was used with the older meaning of 'to be attached.' The people of King James' day knew exactly what Paul was saying. Today that meaning of touch is only used in welding circles.

Here is a further list of Greek words with their sound changes, the original, or older meanings, and the present significance. Now search for your 'shiboleths.' For example, the Hebrew 'shalom' is the Syrian 'salom' and the English 'salem.' This speaks of serenity. Note l to r and m to n change. Greek, ειρηνη = peace, serenity.

1. Γινωσκω= I am growing in knowledge of ; I am becoming intimate.

Greek without Tears

GREEK WORDS	CHANGED	OLD MEANING	PRESENT MEANING
Βαθυς	bassy	base, bass	deep of voice; deep
Βαλλω	ball	throw	cast, heave cf. ballastics

Note: εγω = *ego*—I

Βεβηλος	ve(ry) veal	very vile	profane, unholy, etc.
βια	vis	vim	force, violence
βλασφημια	blasphemy	blasphemy	to speak irreverently (of God); to curse
βους	bov or bof	bovine	= beef made an ox, bull or cow
γαστηρ	gastear	belly	stomach, cf gastric juice in the stomach
γλωσσα	glossa or glotta		a language a language cf. di-glot
γραυς	gray	greyish	oldish one
Heb. 4:13 γυμνος gym	gymned	lightly clad as in clothing	a destitute of proper
τραχηλιζομαι	streak	made streaked	be laid bare or exposed

Greek—Babel or Science of Sound Changes?

γυνη	ginny (Jamaican woman; female donkey)[2]		
δαιμων	demon	demon	evil angel
δακρυω	da cry ego	I give a cry	weep, shed tears
δανος	danos	thing given cf.	gift or loan, which is
Latin do—I give	almost a gift, donation		
δελεαζω	dele az o	I cause delusion	I bait or entice
δερω	tear (δέρμ̈)	I (tear the skin) skin	scorge, flayouter skin
	cf. epi der-mis		
δεω	tie	I tie	bind, hinder
δημος	teamos	the team	the people
δουλος	toilos	toiler	servant, slave
εγκρυπτω	en crypt	to hide in	to intermix

Note γ takes the sound n before γ κ ξ χ i.e. before g, k, x and ch.

αγγελ	angel	angel	angel, messenger
εγκαταλειπω	en/kata/leiv/o	I leave down in	to abandon, leave behind
εγκοπτω	en cot o	I cut in	interrupt, impede, hinder
ειδολον	idol	idol, a doll	image of a god

2. *gyne*; cf. Gynecology.

Greek without Tears

εισπορευομαι	eis poreu mai	I am going forward	I am visiting or entering into, I am boring in
ελκος	ulcos	ulcer	sore

Note the *e* changed to u.

ελλογεω	en log eo	I am logging in	to enter into an account, To record
'ημερα	heam era	hemmed or enclosed	day period of time
ησυχιος	easy chios	easy	quiet, peaceful
θεος	deos	deity	a god, God
θυγατηρ	dugateer	daughter	daughter
'ισχυς	huschys	huskiness	strength, power
καυτηριας ω	cauteriazo	I cauterize	brand, sear
κοιτη	cotea	coitus	cot, bed, sexual intercourse
λαρυγξ	larynx	larynx	throat

HAPPY RELABELLING!

CHAPTER 4

GREEK PRESENT TENSE

"Every speech sound has a meaning." This principle laid down by the Apostle Paul in 1 Corinthians 14:10 will be applied in this chapter in discussing the present tense of Greek verbs ending with ω e.g., λεγω and λυω.

The present active indicative of λυω varies its endings to produce the following meanings:

λύω	Loose I or I am loosing
λύεις	loose you (sing.) or you are loosing
λύει	looses he (she or it) or he (she or it) is loosing or he looses
λύομεν	loose we or we are loosing
λύετε	loose you (pl) or you are loosing
λύουσι	loose they or they are loosing

The sound λυ is constant and is called the stem. This means 'loose.' The endings vary, but these have meanings as well.

15

Greek without Tears

ω	I
εις	you (sing.)
ει	he, she or it
ομεν	we
ετε	You (pl)
ουσι	they

Thus, if we know that λεγω means 'I say,' it follows that the other numbers and persons of λεγω are as follows:-

λεγ-εις	you are saying (sing.)
λέγ-ει	He, she or it is saying
λέγ-ο-μεν	we are saying
λέγ-ε-τε	you are saying (pl.)
λέγ-ουσι	they are saying

The Greek form uses the present continuous almost always. Sometimes because of the nature of the word, the simple present is used e.g., I say, you say etc.

The idea of continuity contained in the Greek present tense can often be expressed by a line _____, and it is said to be linear in action. Some of the other tenses e.g., Aorist, speak of action at a fixed hour, and can be represented by a dot ., and it is said to be punctiliar in action.

If we know the 1st person, singular number, present Indicative Active of a verb, e.g., λεγω, the other persons and numbers can be found by subtracting the ending ω and supplying the appropriate endings to the stem λεγ.

Greek Present Tense

Here are some Greek words ending in ω with their meaning as well as helps in remembering them.

Lexical Study

Βαλλω	I throw (BALListic)
Βλεπω	I see (an abbreviation of I cast an eye. cf OPTic
γινωσκω	I know (ginoo-know a guttural change sk shows approach as in adolescence, more properly then, I am coming to know or I am knowing.
γραφω	I write (I grave. Writing was engraving. To write it upon the heart was a much stronger metaphor then.
εγειρω	I raise (e.g., possibly ek + eir = I air out)
ευρισκω	I find (heuristic)
εχω	I have (I ech cf hitch to, i.e. to hold. Hence, more exactly to have and to hold, to possess (Spanish tener not haber. Latin teneo.)
θεραπεω	I heal. (therapy)
κρινω	I judge. (cf. dis criminate, critic. Note liquid change n to m.
λαμβανω	I take, receive
λεγω	I say
μενω	I remain (= main; hence, to maintain ones position, abide)
πεμπω	I send (= pimp, i.e., to send to get)
σωζω	I save, deliver (literally, I cause to live)

Greek without Tears

EXERCISES

Translate the following:

Πεμπει

Μενομεν

Λεγεις

Κρινουσι

Εχετε

Βαλλει

Γραφεις

Βλεπω

Εγειρομεν

Λαμβανουσι

Θεραπευομεν

Σωζουσι

κρινεις

Chapter 5

GREEK—CIRCUMSTANCES ALTER CASES

The variations of a Greek Noun, Pronoun, Article or Qualifier, are according to case and must be carefully learned. These have great significance in the Greek.

In Act 9:7 and Acts 22:9, Paul makes two statements re his conversion, which seem contradictory. In the first, he said his co-persecutors heard the voice. In the second he said they did not hear the voice. The problem is resolved when we examine the case of "voice." The first in genitive, i.e. 'of the voice.' The second is ACCUSATIVE, i.e. 'to the voice.' The fact is, they hearkened of the voice, but they did not hearken to the voice. They probably went on persecuting Christians.

REVISE THE CASES

Exercise A

What case would you use to translate the nouns and pronouns in the following sentences:

John 2:23 As then he was in *Jerusalem* (in) at the *Passover*, (in) at the *feast many* believed on *his* name viewing *his signs* which he did.

Exercise B

Check your answers at John 2:23. Note Jerusalem, Passover, Feast, as well as their accompanying 'the's' are locative because they tell where he was.

Many is Nominative

His is Genitive (name) of him, (signs) of him.

Name is accusative, telling on what they believed.

Exercise C

Memorize carefully the forms of the Definite Article THE:

	Singular			Plural		
	M.	F.	N.	M.	F.	N.
Nominative	ʽο	ʽη	το	ʽοι	ʽαι	τα
Genitive	του	της	του	των	των	των
Dative	τω	τη	τω	τοις	ταις	τοις
Accusative	τον	την	το	τους	τας	τα

Greek—Circumstances Alter Cases

Answer the following questions based on this form or paradigm.

(i) Where is the "t" omitted? (ii) What is added where the "t" is omitted? (iii) What vowel is always in the Dative Case? (iv) Where is the "i" placed in the singular? (v) What kind of e's and o's are in the Dative Singular (compound)? (vi) What is the ending of the genitive plural in all genders? (vii) What letter is persistent in the feminine gender? (Consider η as ea, ω as oa.) (viii) what letter is persistent in the masculine gender? cf Most Spanish masculine nouns end in "o" and most Spanish feminine nouns end in "a." (ix) What is the Neuter Nominative and Accusative Singular of "the"? (x) What is the Neuter Nominative and Accusative Plural of "the"?

Exercise D

Pick out all the "the's" in Mathew 1:1-6, and tell their number, gender and case.

Learn the meaning of the following words taken from the passage:

γενεσεως	of beginning (cf. Genesis- Book of beginnings)
'υιος	son (cf. *hijo* = son (Sp) *hujo* or *uío* (Gk).
δε	then (Note dental change d to th, and the liquid n slid away.
εκ	out of (cf expel = to throw out of
εγεννησεν	begat (cf root γεν with begin. The ε in front shows past time, just as is often done in English by adding "ed")
αυτου	of himself (cf automobile, automatic)
και	in addition, and, even, also, plus

Greek without Tears

βασιλεα   king, boss" (cf Basilika—a place fit for a king) Most cathedrals in Europe are called Basilikas.

αλδεφους   brothers, cf. Philadelphia-brotherly love

Exercise E

Read and translate Matthew 1:1–6 from your Greek New Testament. If you made it, praise the Lord. If you did not, revise this chapter and try again. You have made it this time I am sure.

Exercise F

With the help of your dictionary Translate Mt. 1:7–11 and John 1:1–15

Chapter 6

GREEK PREFIXES AND INFIXES AS TIME DETERMINANTS

Early grammarians were keenly interested in letters. Intended time was shown by changing the root as in English, e.g., grow—grew and by adding letters before (prefixes) or after the root (suffixes); then would follow the personal endings.

In English, "ed" is added to some verbs to show past time, e.g., weaken—weakened. In Greek an ϵ is placed before the root to show past time, e.g., λυ—loosing, ϵλυ—was loosing or loosed.

Perfect, that is, completed action was shown in the Active Voice by reduplicating the initial letter of the root and followed by 'k' after the root. Example: , λυ—loosing, λϵλυκ has/have loosed.

"s" was placed after the root to show future time, but when the root had also the prefix ϵ it showed action that took place at a fixed point in time (hour). This is called the Aorist tense. Example: λυσ- shall loose (future); ϵλυσ- did loose (aorist) λυθη—shall be loosed.

The Aorist Passive prefixes an ϵ followed by θη after the root. Example: ϵλυθη—was loosed.

The perfect Passive reduplicates, but is not followed by κ. Example: λελυκα—I have loosed

λελυμαι—I have been loosed. (Note personal endings differ).

Here then is a summary of the use of letters to modify tenses (main).

ACTIVE VOICE INDICATIVE MOOD

Tense	Prefix	Root	Infix	Type of Personal Ending
Present	None	Constant	None	Later ω, εις, ει, ομεν, ετε, ουσι as above
Future	None		σ	
Imperfect	ε	Constant	None	
Aorist	ε	Constant	σ	
Perfect	Dup + ε	Constant	κ	ον, ες, ε(ν), ομεν, ετε, ον.

PASSIVE INDICATIVE

Tense	Prefix	Root	Infix	Type of Personal Endings
Present	None	Same	None	ομαι η εται ομεθα εσθε ονται
Future	"	"	—	As Above
Imperfect	—		None	ομην ου ετο ομεθα εσθε οντο
Aorist	—		—	ν ς μεν τε σαν
Perfect	Dup. +ε		None	μαι σαι μεθα σθε νται

Note Infixes in the Passive use θη.

Greek Prefixes and Infixes as Time Determinants

Translate the following verbs:

βαλλει

βαλλομεν

θεραπευσω

ελυε

ελυσας

λελυκαμεν

λυεσθε

λυθησαμεθα

ελυομην

ελυθημεν

λελυνται

Put into Greek: he has been loosed, they were being loosed. They were loosed. He shall be loosed. He is being loosed. You (pl.) are healing. He shall heal. I was healing. He did heal. He has loosed.

Check your tables to see how well you did.

Additional Notes for Irregular Verbs:

(i) Where the root begins with a vowel:

prefix ε combines with ε or α to form η

Prefix ε combines with ο to form ω

η ω ι υ remain unchanged (For example Present αγ̑ γελω Imperfect ηγγελον).

(ii) Where the root begins with a ρ the ρ is doubled before the addition of ε, e.g.. Present ριπτω Imperfect ερριπτον.

(iii) If the last letter of a root is a consonant,

the Labials π β φ π τ combine with S to form ψ.

the Gutterals κ γ χ and σ σ combine with S to form σ.

(iv)   Words with vowel stems ending in ε α ο are lengthened before the addition of the infix σ; e.g., τιμαω—τιμησω ε α become η=εα; ο becomes ω =οα (excepting καλεω τελεω εαω, e.g., future καλεσω).

Roots ending in a Liquid alter their roots but do not infix σ

e.g., Present βαλλω αιρω

Future βαλω αρω

Exercise: Begin reading John's Gospel with the help of your lexicon.

Remember: Translate the Active Tenses Thus:

Present, Future, Imperfect, Aorist, Perfect respectively.

e.g., theVerb to loose, I am loosing, you (sing) are loosing, he, she or it is loosing etc. ; I shall loose; I was loosing, I loosed; I have loosed.

Passive Voce in order: I am being loosed, I shall be loosed, I was being loosed. I was loosed, I have been loosed. N.B.—The emphasis on "being" in the Passive. Exception the Aorist.

CHAPTER 7

PREFIXES

Prefixes, other than those which tell the time of an action, were mainly prepositions, adjectives and nouns. Occasionally an adverb, e.g., ευ = well, was combined with a verb, e.g., ευδοκεω = I think, to form ευδοκεω = I think well. However, because the prepositions outnumber the other forms of prefixes, we should look at some of these, noting their literal meanings, derived meanings and meanings in combination with other words.

Prefix	Literally	Derived Meaning	Combined	Meaning Combined
κατα	down	against	κατανοεω	I understand
καταλυω				I demolish
απω	off, from	away, aside	αποβαλλω	I cast away
δια	twain	through, between	διακρινω	I distinguish
εις	into	towards	εισελθειν	to go into
εν	in	in, at, with	εγκοπτω	I cut in, I interrupt
εκ	out of	from, out	εκβαινω	I go out from

Greek without Tears

επι	upon	over, on	επιβαλλω	I throw upon
μετα	mix	change, with, after	μετατιθημι	I transfer, i.e make a change
περι	around	about	περιπατεω	I walk about
προ	fore	forth, ahead	προγραφω	I write beforehand
προσ	front	facing towards with	προσφερω	I bear to, -offer
συν	together with	along with together	συμφωνος	Agree together in sound

Look in your dictionary for these prepositions combined with other roots, as well as the following:

παρα = beside along 'υπερ = over, super, upper, over for

'υπο = under, sub   αντι = at the end of, opposite, instead of

Examples of adjectives which have been used as prefixes to alter the meaning of the root are:

δυσ = dys, bad, e.g., δυσεντερια dysentery, i.e. bad interior (intestine)

'ετερο = other 'ετερογλωσσος other language

ισος = equal ισοτιμος equal esteemed, of equal price

μακρο = far, long μακροχρονιος long time, long lived

πολυ = many much πολυτιμος much esteemed, of much value

νεος = new νεοφυτος newly planted, novice

Examples of nouns in combination are:

γη = earth γεογραφια writing about the earth, geography

θεος = god θεοδιδακτος taught of God

Note, chiropodist is a hand–foot specialist.

Prepositions are very important in the Greek and should be carefully noted as they sometimes dominate the meanings of the words when they are in combination with other roots, e.g., καταλυω I loose thoroughly or down.

Translate Luke 6:1, 6, 12

Examine the meanings of other words with these prefixes

Examples: καταστροφη απολειπω διασωζω εισακουω.

CHAPTER 8

AGREEMENT OR CONCORD

Let us next deal with the fundamental agreements that are found in all developed languages. These are essential for accuracy of translation.

1. Adjectives agree with the nouns they qualify in Number, Gender and Case. Its agreement is trifold. E.g., "good man" is put in the Greek five different ways, depending on the circumstance. (case).

    If "good man" is the subject or nominative, it is αγαθος ανθροπως.

    If it is vocative case, i.e. addressing him it is αγαθε ανθρωπε.

    If it is accusative i.e., action taking place on him, it is αγαθον ανθροπων.

    If it is Dative, i.e. taking place to, for , by or near him it is αγαθω ανθροπω.

    If the "good man" possesses something, it is Genitive αγαθου ανθροπου.

Agreement or Concord

Of course, if the Gender or Number of the noun changes the adjective changes.

2. Verbs are also changed according to their circumstances in five ways, according to their Number, Person, Voice, Mood and Tense. This we saw in the study of Prefixes and Suffixes as Time Determinants.
3. The cases of nouns following certain prepositions vary according to circumstances.

Note the examples following which use the abbreviations A, G, D for Accusative, Genitive and Dative respectively.

Class (a) Prepositions which take only one Case.

(i) Where the meaning logically includes the idea of "of" it is Genitice e.g., αντι.

αντι—instead of, at the end of; απο away from; εκ, εξ, out of, from inside. προ in front of.

Where its meaning includes the idea of motion to or back, it is Accusative. E.g., ανα

up again, εις, into, toward.

(ii) Where its meaning includes agreement, location or agency, it is Dative,

συν   together; ἐν, in on, by, with.

Class (b) Prepositions which take either Gen, Acc, or Dat.

Here the basic meanings of the preposition, taken together with the basic ideas contained in the case, are helpful in arriving at the true meaning.

E.g.,   παρα with Genetive/Ablative   = along from, from.
        παρα   Accusative   = along towards, toward.
        παρα   Dative = along at, close by.

επι with Genitive = up of, i.e. on, over.
επι with accusative = up to i.e. unto.
επι with Dative = up to i.e. upon.
προς with Genitive = towards of i.e. for, on behalf of.
προς with Accusative = towards to i.e. towards, with.
προς with Dative = towards at i.e. close by.

Class (c) Prepositions which take either Genitive or Accusative.

Where δια (through) means 'by means' of it takes the Genitive.

Where it means 'due to,' 'on account of,' it take the Accusative.

Where κατα = down means down from or against, it takes the Genitive.

Where it means down to or according to, it takes the Accusative.

Where μετα = in the midst of, with, it takes the Genitive.

Where μετα = toward the midst of, after, it takes the Accusative.

Where περι = around of, concerning, it takes the Genitive.

Where περι = around about (action) it takes the Accusative.

'υπερ = over and 'υπο—under are respectively over of, under of, i.e. on behalf of and under the hand of take the Genitive Over to—above and under to below take the Accusative.

OTHER AGREEMENTS are as follows:

1. The complements of the verb 'to be' agree with the subject in Number, Gender and Case (John 1:19).
2. Participles agree with the Nouns they qualify in number gender and case (John 1:26).

Agreement or Concord

3. Relative Pronouns take their own case, but take their number and gender from the nouns to which they relate, John 1:26.

NEGATIVES are chosen to show facts (ου = not) or possibility (μη John 3:5).

Unfulfilled conditions are negated by μη, hence found with Imperative, Subjective, and Optative (John 3:7).

Never use μη μη, use μη ου. This is a double negative, which does not cancel as in English, but is emphatic, and can be translated 'by no means!' (Mt. 16:22).

μη in a question expects the answer No (1 Corinthians 12: 29).

ου in a question expects the answer Yes (Luke 17:17).

Did you associate with walk. i.e. walking of your own accord? Then you can see why the word is translated sometimes "come" and sometimes "go." It all depends on the context.

CHAPTER 9

EVERY SPEECH SOUND HAS A MEANING

Sounds worth noting in word building

a). The preposition and personal endings have already been noted.

b). Word endings with ικος = suitable for, apt, designed for.

  βασιλικος = befitting or worthy of a king or boss James 2:8.

  διδακτικος (didactic) . = apt to teach, fit for teaching 1 Tim 3:2

  πνευματικος = fit for, adapted to or suitable for the Spirit (1 Cor. 12:1)   cf σαρκικος fit for the flesh.

c). ινος = made of

  σαρκινος = made of flesh cf earthen, saline (made of salt) .

  cf. σαρκος = of flesh, fleshy Rom 9:8cf 1 Cor 3:1, 3.

Every Speech Sound has a Meaning

d). ιζω   = cause or make to.

     βαπτιζω   = cause or make to dip John 4:1,2.

     μετοικιζω   = make a house change, to emigrate Acts 7:4.

e). εσκω   = to approach.

     θησκω = to approach death, I am dying, rather than I die.

     cf. adolescent—approaching adulthood.

f). ισμος   (having the effect of (cf. capital*ism*, social*ism*).

g). της   = one who practices.   Ποιητης = one who practices to do, a performer, composer.

h). Endings which are noun forming.

     ον   = a place, station, or thing.

     βιβλιον   = a thing billed or booked i.e. a book or record.

     μα   = matter or thing e.g., doma, a thing given, a gift.

     ια ις η   = act or state of.

     πορνεια   = act or porning, fornication, immorality.

     γενεσις   = beginning, birth, cf crisis—critical stage.

     υπομονη   = remaining under, endurance, perseverance.

i). Sounds which are adjective forming e.g., ιος.

     γυναικειος   = pertaining to a woman, female 1 Peter 3:7.

j). Sounds which are adverb forming ως.

     ισος ισως   = equal adj. equally adv. respectively.

     κατα καθως   = according to, accordingly "(just as) respectively.

Find and note other examples of these special sounds 1 Cor 14:10.

EVERY SPEECH SOUND (φωνη) HAS A MEANING.

CHAPTER 10

PARTICIPLES AND THEIR USES

PARTICIPIAL ENDINGS

The following endings preceded by the stem to form the various participles.

PRESENT TENSE ACTIVE

	Singular				Plural		
	Masc.	Fem.	Nuet.		Masc.	Fem.	Neut.
Nom.	ων	ουσα	ον		οντες	ουσαι	οντα
Acc.	οντα	ουσαν	ον		οντας	ουσας	οντα
Gen.	οντας	ουσης	οντας		οντων	ουσων	οντων
Dat.	οντι	ουση	οντι		ουσι	ουσαις	ουσι

Note in the Singular the dominance of the 't' in the masculine and neuter; the dominance of the ουσ in the feminine; and the dominance of 's' in the ending of the Genitive.

Participles and Their Uses

Note: In the plural οντ is dominant except where it is followed by an 's' as with the Feminine endings. Here the t and n vanish and are compensated by a'u' e.g., Dative Plural of λυω (λυουσι), not λυοντσι masc or neuter. Since 's' will not follow 't or n' in Greek. Note 'i' is always in the Dative Case.

The present participle is used where the action takes place at the same time as the main verb. ὁ ἔχων δύο χιτῶνας μεταδότω τῷ μὴ ἔχοντι (The one having two coats let him share with the one not having). Note the case of the one having and that of the one not having.

AORIST TENSE ACTIVE

CASE	Singular			Plural		
	Masc.	Fem.	Nuet.	Masc.	Fem.	Neut.
Nom.	σας	σασα	σαν	σαντες	σασαι	σαντα
Acc.	σαντα	σασαν	σαν	σαντας	σασας	σαντα
Gen.	σαντος	σασης	σαντος	σαντων	σασων	σαντων
Dat.	σαντι	σαση	σαντι	σασι	σασαις	σασι

Study carefully the Nominative Masculine Singular. To get the other Aorist forms from the Present, replace the initial vowels 'o' or 'ou' by sa e.g., Nom, Fem, Present of λυω is λυουσα but the Aorist is λυσασα (Sing.) or λυουσαι (Plur.), respectively.

Participles being partly verbs and partly adjectives differ from regular verbs mainly in their endings. Instead of personal endings, case endings are used.

The case endings of the present tense follow that of ων.

The case endings of the Aorist tense follow that of σας.

The case endings of the Middle and Passive are like e.g., αγαθος (os) e.g., λυομενος, η, ον.

37

USES OF THE PARTICIPLE

The main uses of the participle are as follows:

a). As a verbal noun e.g., ὁ πιστευων, the believer, the one believing.

b). To show the relationship of a subordinate clause to a main clause: Ἀναστὰς δὲ ἀπὸ τῆς συναγωγῆς εἰσῆλθεν εἰς τὴν οἰκίαν. The having risen from the synagogue he went into the house.

c). To complete the sense with the verb to be (ειμι) e.g., Καὶ ἦν κηρύσσων (and he was preaching).

d). To show the circumstances existing at the time of the action of the main verb, although the action may have taken place independently of the subject or object of the main verb. Here the noun or pronoun and the participle are placed in the GENITIVE CASE (Latin Ablative)). Note Greek Genitive and Ablative have the same form: Δύνοντος δὲ τοῦ ἡλίου ... ἤγαγον αὐτοὺς πρὸς αὐτόν (With the sun setting ... they brought them to him/ when the sun was setting, ... they them to him). Note the Genitive of the sun and setting. These describe the circumstances under which the people ('they') acted.

Exercises

Translate the following verses from your Greek New Testament:

John 3:15, 21, 36; John 4:51; John 5:19, 24, 25; John 6:14; John 6:37, 39, 40, 59, 60.

Pick out the participles in John 5:29. State the number, gender, case and tense of each, then translate. Do the same with Acts 19:2; Ephesians 1:13, John 3:31 and John 6:35.

CHAPTER 11

THE SUBJUNCTIVE MOOD

This is the mood which expresses something for the sake of argument, a supposition, a doubt, a fear, a purpose or an unfulfilled condition.

It reminds us of a clergyman who spoke so hesitantly about everything, that his sermons were characterized by 'a's. Like the Scribes he was unsure of everything.

In the Greek "a" is persistent in the Subjunctive, if we interpret η as ea and ω as oa. This "a" sound is found just after the stem or after the infix following the stem. This is illustrate by comparing the present INDICATIVE Active of λύω with the Present SUBJUNCTIVE Active as follows:

	Indicative	Subjunctive	Notes
1	λύω	λύω	
2	λύεις	λύῃς	(Note ε becomes η)
3	λύει	lu,h|	
1	λύομεν	λύωμεν	(Note o becomes ω)

Greek without Tears

2	λύετε	λύητε	
3	λύουσι(ν)	λύωσι(ν)	(Note ου becomes ω)

Note that where there is already an η/ ω in the indicative, there is no change required in the Subjuntive.

In the Aorist tense the e- prefix is dropped in the subjunctive since this mood does not refer to events that have happened.

There are special conjunctions which are used to introduce clauses whose verbs are in the subjunctive e.g., ινα and οπως which indicate purpose, and εαν, αν, οταν, εως which indicate doubt or uncertainty.

Remember the indicative asserts a fact.

Was Christ stating a fact in John 21:22,23. Read from the Greek cf 1 Cor 13:1,2.

Note, too that the negative of the Subjuntive is μη, expect after verbs of fearing when ου is used. μη is used after a verb of fearing which is positive.

Translate the following noting that ει means if as a fact, but εαν means if ever or even if. 1 John 3:22; 1 John 4:7; 1 John 5:16, John 15:27; John 14:15; John 8:16 1 Cor 14:1,5.

If you have translated all these passages from the Greek. You would have understood clearly our Lord's insistence that he did not say that John would tarry until he come, but even if 'ean' he wished him to do so, What is that to you? A mere hypothetical conjecture. Do not make the same mistake as Peter.

CHAPTER 12

HAVING FUN WITH NUMBERS AND THE INFINITIVE MOOD AS WELL

HERE ARE THE CARDINALS WHICH TELL THE NUMBER:

One	εἷς (masc.) μία (fem) ἕν (neut.) Note Neut. Form nearest to the English *an* i.e. one.
Two	δύο Note dental change *d* for *t*
Three	τρεῖς, τρια (neut.) Neut. Form nearest to Eng.
Four	τέσσαρες cf. Latin t*etra*
Five	πέντε cf. pentagon
Six	ἕξ (hex) cf. hexagon (six angles of corners) Lat. Sex.
Seven	ἑπτά (hepta) Note ' acting as an apostrophe = S here. Cf. Septuagint and ἑσπερ where it = V, Vesper.
Eight	ὀκτώ cf. octagon

Greek without Tears

Nine	ἐννέα
Ten	δέκα one deck; cf. decalogue
Eleven	ἕνδεκα one + ten (Matt 28:16)
Twelve	δώδεκα two + ten (Acts 6:2)
Thirteen	δεκατρεῖς 3+ten
Fourteen	δεκατεσσαες
Fifteen	δέκαπεντε
Twenty	εικοσι a score
Thirty	τριακοντα three counts
Forty	τεσσαρακοντα four counts
Fifty	πεντεκοντα five counts (pentecost)
Sixty	ἕξηκοντα six counts
Seventy	ἑβδουμηκοντα Note the double shift *pt* to *bd*

Here are the first twelve ordinals which tell the ORDER: Note the endings tos or os is an adjectival ending and is declined like adjectives of the first and 2nd declension e.g., αγαθος (good).

πρῶτος, η, ον	First, in front, before
δεύτερος	Second cf. Deuteronomy 2nd giving of the Law
τρίτος	Third
τέταρτος	Fourth. Note change from *ss* to *t* in the ordinal
πέμπτος	Fifth Note μπ replaces ν (replaces by English V in five)
ἕκτος	Sixth Note change from ξ to κ
ἕβδομος	Seventh
ογδοος	Eight. Note change from *kt* in the cardinals
ενατος	Ninth
δεκατος	Tenth
ενδεκατος	Eleventh
δωδεκατος	Twelfth

Examine the declensions of the following declinable cardinals.

Having Fun with Numbers and the Infinitive Mood as well

a.	Masc.	Fem.	Neuter
Nom.	εἷς	μία	ἕν
Acc.	ἕνα	μίαν	ἕν
Gen.	ἑνός	μιᾶς	ἑνός
Dat.	ἑνί	μιᾷ	ἑνί

b.	Masc.	Fem.	Neuter
Nom.	δύο	δύο	δύο
Acc.	δύο	δύο	δύο
Gen.	δυσί	δυσί	δυσί
Dat.	δυσί	δυσί	δυσί

c.	Masc.	Fem.	Neuter
Nom.	τρεῖς	τρεῖς	τρία
Acc.	τρία	τρία	τρία
Gen.	τριῶν	τριῶν	τριῶν
Dat.	τρισί(ν)	τρισί(ν)	τρισί(ν)

d.	Masc.	Fem.	Neuter
Nom.	τέσσαρες	τέσσαρες	τέσσαρα
Acc.	τέσσαρας	τέσσαρας	τέσσαρα
Gen.	τεσσάρων	τεσσάρων	τεσσάρων
Dat.	τέσσαρσι(ν)	τέσσαρσι(ν)	τέσσαρσι(ν)

Note the numeral εἷς (μία ἕν) is compounded with ουδε and μηδε to form ουδεις, μηεις etc. Note where two e's meet, one is usually dropped (elided); cf. ουδεμια = not even one. One is only used for emphasis, since "a" or "an" is assumed in the Singular noun. Translate Mark 25:15; 2:7; Rev 6:1,3,5,7,9,12; 7:1.

43

HOW TO RECOGNIZE THE INFINITIVE MOOD

This mood carries two endings -ειν and -αι. Together they form the present infinitive of the verb to be i.e., ειναι. Thus, to loose (habitually is λυειν (linear) Act. Pres. to loose (particularly) λυσαι, (punctiliar); Aorist, to be loosed (continuously) λυεσθαι (Linear Pass. Pres). to be loosed (at a point in time λυθεναι (Passive Aorist).

Note the ending is either -ειν or -αι. The distinction is in the infix, which comes between the stem and the ending.

θην and εσθαi show Passive or Middle S before ειν show future σ before αι shows Aorist.

Note there is no e prefix before the Aorist, since it merely indicates the type of action.

Translate the following verses:

John 3:2; Matt 27:12; John 3:14; Luke 10:38

Note that the present infinitive suggests continuous, habitual or repeated action

Translate: δει θυγατριον ελθειν (Aorist Infinitive) νυν.

Βούλομαι οὖν προσεύχεσθαι τοὺς ἄνδρας . . . ωαύτως καὶ γυναῖκας . . . διδάσκειν δὲ γυναιxὶ οὐx ἐπιτρέπω.

Chapter 13

VOWEL CONTRACTIONS—CRASIS

Verbs which have their stems ending in e, a, or o, have sometimes to be joined with vowels which connect them to their personal endings. The results of this marriage union is set out in the table below: e.g., e + suffix o= ou

Vowels in Suffixes

	ει (inf.) ε, ε	ει (other)	ε	η	ῃ	ο	ου	ω
Final	ε	ει	ει	ει	η	ῃ	ου	ου	ω
Stem	α	α	ᾳ	α	α	ᾳ	ω	ω	ω
Vowels	ο	ου	οι	ου	ω	οι/ῳ	ου	ου	ω

It is necessary to study these in order to conjugate verbs whose stems end in e, a, or o e.g., τιμαω.

The order of dominance is male dominated. That is, if we take o to represent the male (cf. Spanish noun endings generally) and I to represent that which is male like, we will find that o and I are never lost in any combination, except in the infinitive where the 'i' was originally an 'e.' 'e' which is neutral is the first to go when the going gets tough i.e. when it meets upon a dipthong (double vowel) or upon a semi-dipthong (double or lengthened letter e.g., η ω).

Bearing this in mind the following rules will apply in the marriage contracts:

1. α will not marry ε nor η, but readily joins with o to form ω and with ι to form α.
2. ε + ε ει except in infinitives
3. o says yes to α and ι and η but with ε it says ου i.e., 'O you,' not 'you.'

To illustrate the preceding, let us write the present tense of φιλεω in its uncontracted form on the left and in the usual contracted form on the right. The result is:

Present Active Indicative

S	1.	φιλέ-ω	φιλῶ
	2.	φιλέ-εις	φιλεῖς
	3.	φιλέ-ει	φιλεῖ
Pl	1.	φιλέ-ομεν	φιλοῦμεν
	2.	φιλέ-ετε	φιλεῖτε
	3.	φιλέ-ουσι	φιλοῦσι

Present Passive[1] Indicative

S	2.	φιλέου	φιλοῦ
	3.	φιλέεσθω	φιλείσθω
Pl	2.	φιλέεσθε	φιλεῖσθε
	3.	φιλεέσθωσαν	φιλείσθωσαν

1. Or Middle.

Vowel Contractions—Crasis

Present Active Imperative

S	2.	(φίλεε)	φίλει
	3.	(φιλεέτω)	φιλείτω
Pl	2.	(φιλέετε)	φιλεῖτε
	3.	(φιλεέτωσαν)	φιλείτωσαν

Using the tables for the contraction of Vowels, write out the following verb forms at first uncontracted and then contracted: The Active Present Indicative, Subjunctive, Imperative and Infinitive of τηρεω, τιμαω, φανεροω.

Do the same for the Passive Voice Present Tense.

The technical term for the marriage of two vowels when they meet is 'crasis' i.e., a mixing. και is sometimes contracted with εγω, εαν, εκεινος, εκει, to form καγω, καν, κακεινος, κακει, respectively.

CHAPTER 14

CONDITIONAL CLAUSES

"If you study this lesson carefully, you will understand it." Here I have stated a condition, which, if carried out in the future, will lead to an understanding.

"If you study this lesson carefully "we will call the "if clause" or the clause which tells the condition. Grammarians call this protasis, that which is set out beforehand. Theologians have differed for centuries over whether God has set out beforehand a condition for our salvation. Has he?

"You will understand it "is the "then clause" the result of apodosis. (that which is given back)

There are basically four types of Conditional Sentences:

    a). Those indicating. A condition or supposition of fact in the Past or Present Tense. These take εἰ and the indicative in the "if clause"

Conditional Clauses

E.g., ἐι αὐτὸν θέλω μένειν ἕως ἔρχομαι, τί πρὸς σέ; (If I wish him to remain until I come, what is that to you [yu]?).[1] Note the verb is indicative here.

b). Those supposing a future possibility in the future. These take εαν ἐὰν and the subjunctive e.g., ἐὰν αὐτὸν θέλω μένειν ἕως ἔρχομαι, τί πρὸς σέ; This means, If ever or even if I may wish him to remain until I come... (Read John 21:22-23 and see the reason for the misunderstanding).

c). Those expressing a supposition of extreme doubt, Here is followed by the optative mood in the "if clause" Here means if (and I doubt it very much e.g., 1 Peter 3:14. Here Peter doubts whether we are reproached for the sake of righteousness

d). Those expressing a supposition contrary to fact. Here ει is followed by the indicative in the "if clause" but note the αν in the "then clause" e.g., εἰ ὁ θεὸς πατὴρ ὑμῶν ἦν ἠγαπᾶτε ἂν ἐμέ (lit. If God were your father [and he is not] you would have loved me). Note here the αν = would. It governs the verb. Where it governs the noun or pronoun, as in its compound form. Think of it as 'ever or even.'

As is customary, the negative ου is used with the Indicative, and μη is used with the subjunctive.

Exercise: Translate the following verses noting the Tenses and the Mood used in the clauses.

Matt 4:3,6; 5:29,30; 19:10, 16. 1 Tim 2:15, John 6:62, 1 Cor 13:1,2,3; 1 Cor 2:8, 15:16; Acts 19:2. Note that in the latter case, because the 'if clause' is in the indicative, the 'if' can be translated 'since,' with the meaning: 'since as you say 'not with the meaning 'from the time that. Distinguish between the conditional 'since' and the temporal 'since'!

Acts 19:2 could therefore be literally rendered; If or since having believed (as you are saying as a fact), have you received the Holy Spirit?

---

1. Literal rendering; *yu*—Jamaican for you singular.

Chapter 15

THIRD DECLENSION

Like Third World Nations, the 3rd declension is non-aligned i.e., they neither belong to the 1st nor 2nd declension.

They are two kinds: those whose stems end in a consonant, and those whose stems end in a vowel. To find the stem ending subtract the ending os from the Genitive singular Thus

Gen. sing	Stem	
λεοντος	λεοντ	Consonant stem
τριχος	τριχ	Consonant stem
πολεως	πολι	Vowel Stem
ιχθος	ιχθυ	Vowel Stem

	Singular		
N.	νύξ	σάρξ	ἄρχων
G.	νυκτός	σαρκός	ἄρχοντος
D.	νυκτί	σαρκί	ἄρχοντι
A.	νύκτα	σάρκα	ἄρχοντα

Third Declension

V.	νύξ	σάρξ	ἄρχων
		Plural	
N.V.	νύκτες	σάρκες	ἄρχοντες
G.	νυκτῶν	σαρκῶν	ἀρχόντων
D.	νυξί(ν)	σαρξί(ν)	ἄρχουσι(ν)
A.	νύκτας	σάρκας	ἄρχοντας

νύξ, ἡ, stem νυκτ-, *a night*

σάρξ, ἡ, stem σαρκ-, *flesh*

ἄρχων, ὁ, stem ἀρχοντ-, *a ruler*

	Singular	
	M. F.	N.
N.	τις	τι
G.	τινός	τινός
D.	τινί	τινί
A.	τινά	Τι
	Plural	
N.	τινές	τινά
G.	τινῶν	τινῶν
D.	τισί(ν)	τισί(ν)
A.	τινάς	τινά

CHAPTER 16

OPTATIVE MOOD & VOCABULARY AIDS

OPTATIVE MOOD

The optative mood is used when we hope or 'opt' for something. It is the mood of wishful thinking e.g., "Would that you were here." The verb to wishfully think in Greek is οιμαι and οι usually comes between the stem and the ending in Greek verbs whenever the expression 'would that' is intended. ει found in the Passive Aorist is best translated 'may that' e.g., 1 Peter 3:14 (ἀλλ' εἰ καὶ πάσχοιτε διὰ δικαιοσύνην, μακάριοι.): "But if, and would that you [unu][1] suffer (very doubtful) for righteousness happy are you."

A Popular example found in Romans 6:15 is μὴ γένοιτο = Would that it may not happen! This hope is often translated in KJV, God forbid.

---

[1]. Jamaican for 'you' plural.

Optative Mood & Vocabulary Aids

Note: In negating a wish, a supposition or a command, μη is used, not ου. After verbs of fearing reverse the usage.

VOCABULARY AIDS

Some Key Letters and Syllables are as follows:

αν= up e.g., ανθρωπος = the upturned one, man.

οι= would that between stem and ending of verbs.

σ= shall ' between stem and ending and without prefix e.g., λυσω (I shall loose).

-εις= Thou

α= "May" when it lengthens the connecting vowel e.g., λυετε (you loose); λυητε (you may loose).

ε= "ed" a past tense prefix e.g., ελυσε (He loosed).

βα= go.

ος= he who is e.g., πιλατος (he who pilots or governs). Later a name.

ευ= well, good e.g., ευλογια (a good word, speech; blessing).

ια= A noun forming abstraction e.g., κοινωνια (fellowship).

σα= sign of Aorist as a rule. Ελυσατε.

ευ= "ing" after the stem e.g., συμβασιλευω (I am reigning together).

So far we have been guessing at the meaning of our Greek stems and checking to see if we have missed the mark. The context of the passage has been a valuable help. Now let us look at our Greek Lexicon and see in what ways we could give the meanings, by associating the words with known English words, or by juggling our consonants according to Ted's Law (See Chapter 3 on Babels.)

Firstly names are easily recognized. There are only slight differences in the spelling e.g., , Αγαβος Agabus.

Secondly, Prefixes alter the meanings of the Stem. Some like α sometimes deprive the stem of its meaning e.g., αβαρης, weightless, and sometimes emphasize the meaning e.g., αγαθος good (virtuous). Note by changing the dental θ for 'd', and ignoring the vowel change, γαθ becomes good.[2]

Thirdly, Rhotacism, the excessive use of 'R' (and its substitution for "S") accounts for the change of spelling e.g., γαρ[3] is in Latin Causa and in English Cause. Faulty pronunciation also leads to Rhotacism e.g., κλαιω (to cry; cf. Oriental Labbi for Rabbit. Note, too, the dropping of the dental at the end).

Fourthly, Metathesis i.e., the change of the position of sounds in a word. e.g., καρπος = crop, fruit. απτομαι = to be fitted; the vowels are ignored.[4] Hence the deponent απτομαι can be translated to be fitted or attached viz. I Cor: 7:1. NIV's "not to be married" has its merits over not to touch (cf. also τασσω, set).

Fifthly, try meditation on the word with the meaning before you. Try to connect the two languages. Even if you fail to do so, the effort would have aided your memory. Besides, you may surprise yourself with the clue. The word εαω is a case in point. Its connection with allow permit etc. is not readily seen. But when it dawns on you that an SE could have been eluded from the original "ease," because of the dislike of an S to stay between two vowels (cf. CAUSE and GAR). Then remembering that an easement is a permit, the meaning becomes clear.

More things are wrought through meditation than this world dreams of.

---

2. Stems when separated from their prefixes can more easily be associated with their roots (Pardon the pun) e.g., a=gam-os = (not gammed or gummed) associate with *gametes*, polygamy, and we get the meaning unmarried.

3. For.

4. Note P.T.= F.T.

OTHER HELPS

P FOR Q. This is due to the absence of Q in later Greek. Thus *quo* (Latin-where) is που in Greek, and *equus* (horse) is ἱππος.

K,C,S., are interchangeable sounds e.g., Kuri (os) Cyrus, Sir, are saying the same thing, a Superior i.e., Lord.

MEMORIZE GEMS: familiar passages as the Lord's Prayer should be memorized.

TRANSLATION: Read a passage from the Greek daily; first a line, then a verse. Soon you will wish to do a chapter or even a Book, from the Book of Books.

These aids will greatly help in removing the boredom of vocabulary study. As one of my tutors once told me. Study with vigour you remember with ease. Study without it goes to the breeze.

Chapter 17

OH MI, OH MAI

Thus far we have seen that the 1st Person Singular, Present Indicative Active of Greek verbs is ended with ω.

Omega in this context means "I." There are, however, a few Greek verbs which substitute μι for μαι, and which are usually causative in effect. Compare Shakespeare's "Me thinks" for "I think." There is a change in the personal pronoun and usually a change in the form of the Stem.

Now let us examine the changes in the personal endings and the stems of the 1st Person, Present Indicative Active Singular of three of the most frequently used of these Mi Verbs.

θεω	=	I put becomes τιθημι I cause to put (Jamaican, *me de put*).
σταω	=	I stand becomes ιστιμι I cause to stand.
δοω	=	I give becomes διδωμι I cause to give.

Note the following differences:

(i) An 'I' is placed before the stem not an 'e' which would indicate past time.

(ii) There is reduplication. In the case of "s" the ' takes its place. Cf. ὑπυρ = Latin Super.

(iii) The vowel is lengthened.

> Other Mi verbs worth noting are:
>
> δεικνυμι = I cause to show from δεικνυω. Here note that the U is not lengthened, nor is there a reduplication + "i." αμφιεννυμι = I cause to be put on, invest, or clothe someone else.
>
> ανατιθημι = I am causing to be put up, i.e. to have submitted.

As shown below, the lengthened vowels are found in the sing. of the present indicative where the changes in the personal endings are marked, but NOT in the plural where the personal endings are still μεν, τε, σι. Because of the similarity of the 3rd pers. sing. and the 3rd pers. plur. Note how the difference is shown below.

	Singular	Plural
1.	τίθημι	τίθεμεν
2.	τίθης	τίθετε
3.	τίθησι(ν)	τιθέασι(ν)

	Singular	Plural
1.	ἵστημι	ἵσταμεν
2.	ἵστης	ἵστατε
3.	ἵστησι(ν)	ἱστᾶσι(ν)

	Singular	Plural
1.	δίδομαι	διδόμεθα
2.	δίδοσαι	δίδοσθε
3.	δίδοται	δίδονται

Greek without Tears

An interesting Mi verb is φιημι = I am saying (emphatically as a prophet. Fay and Say are related. Have you ever noticed the Old English S and its nearness to F?   Remember most MI verbs are causative in effect, cf. -ιζω verbs.

Translate I John 2: 7–11.

Chapter 18

It is now generally accepted by many Greek scholars, that the problems involved in mastering the accent of the ancient Greeks, is not worth it.

Firstly, because accents were not placed in the earliest New Testament Manuscripts.

Secondly, the rules seem t have so many exceptions that they can scarcely be called rules.

Thirdly, because where the experts differ, the student is thrown into confusion.

There are, however, a few cases where differences in accents would throw some light upon the exact meaning of a word.

The following distinctions should be noted. Please note that the absence of an accent could indicate a grave accent or none.

   a). The conjunction ει = if. The verb to be εἴ = you are (sing).
      Cf. Spanish si = 'if'and affirmative *si* = yes.

   b). The preposition εις =   into the numeral εἴς =one.
      The preposition εξ = out of into the numeral ἐξ = six.

   c). Present Tense   μενω= I remain; Future μενῶ =I shall remain.
      Present Tense κρινω= I judge; Future χρινῶ =I shall judge.

d). Indef. Pronoun   s: τις τι=someone, something, and interrogatives: τίς τί who? what?

e). Article   ὁ=the; Relative pron ὅ = that, which.

Article ἡ =the;   the Conjunction ἤ = or, than.[1]

Remember then, distinguish between things that differ. Be accurate in your translation. Read your Greek Testament daily. Be faithful to what God reveals to you, but above all, use it with love—not all are ready for it.

Translate:

- εἰ υἱὸς εἶ τοῦ θεοῦ, βάλε σεαυτὸν κάτω·
- ἡ γυνὴ ἔλεγεν
- τί φάγητε ἢ τί πίητε;

Did you recognize the differences.

Translate Matt. 7: 4, 9–11; John 17:24.

Note carefully how the breathing and the context can be of assistance in solving your problem.

---

1. Or another relative pronoun, ἥ (who; feminine).

Chapter 19

Review—Differences in Expressing Greek and English

1. The Greek verb is really a sentence with the pronoun placed at the end. E.g., γραφ ω   = write I (English I write). Note the reversing of the pronoun in English.
2. Tense is not only used to show time, but the type of action. The aorist—action at a fixed time; the Present almost always continuous or repeated action.
3. The Greek uses a 3rd Voice. In the sentence, John marries Mary. Both are active and both are passive. The Middle Voice would best be used here to show a mutual reciprocal and voluntary activity. A deponent could also be used e.g., απτομαι= I attach myself. See I Cor. 7:1.
4. Case: Only a few case forms are found in English e.g., He, Him, His. Greek uses five forms corresponding to eight English cases. e.g., τῷ ἀνθρώπῳ, to or for the man (dative), in or at the man (locative), or by or with the man (instrumental).

5. Adjectives in Greek agree in number, gender and case with the nouns they qualify.

αγαθον ανθρωπον = a good man (accusative). Adjectives ending in -ικος and -ινος are really descriptive phrases, meaning respectively, fit for the stem or made of the stem. For example, βασιλικος = fit for a king, royal; σαρκινος= made of flesh.

6. Prepositions, in Greek, vary in meaning with the cases e.g., δια προφητειας (gen. sing) = by prophecies but δια προφῆτειας (acc. plur. Note same words) = for the sake of prophecies. Now translate I Timothy 4:14. Which do you think it is?

Prepositions are often combined with the verb for emphasis e.g., λυω = I loose,

καταλυω= I loose down or thoroughly loose.

Prepositions often change their meaning in combination with verbs e.g., μετα = with, after. But μεταβαινω= I go across, transfer. A preposition in combination is often repeated with the noun e.g., εκφερω αρτον εκ του οικου= I bring out bread out of the house. Before a vowel with smooth breathing a preposition drops or elides its ending vowel, eg., επι οικου = ἐποικου.

T and P become th and ph when followed by a rough breathing e.g., αντι ἁμαρτίας = ανθ ἁμαρτίας .

7. Enclitics

In English, we say "The Jesse begat David." Greek says "Jesse then (δε) begat David." δε is said to be an enclitic because it never begins a sentence, but lies within it. There are a few more e.g., = for, = indeed.

8. Possessive Adjectives

English says 'my word,' Greek says, 'the word of me' (ὁ λογος μου).

Review—Differences in Expressing Greek and English

9. The emphatic use of 'the' e.g., The Jesus, and also to show abstractions e.g., The wisdom.
10. Some verbs take different cases e.g., Acts. (:7 Hearkened of the voice (gen.). Acts 22:9 Hearkened to the voice (acc.) Translate these verses and compare with you A.V.
11. δε = then; and και= and, even, also, as well as—are not easy to interpret and must be translated in the light of the context. e.g., τουτο δε και εγω γινωσκω = lit. This then even I myself know, or buth this I also know. και . . . και = both . . . and, even . . . as well as.
12. Participles

These are more used in Greek than in English, and the difference between the aorist and the Present must be noticed. The present participle describes things taking place at the same time as that of the main clause. e.g., *Loosing the ass,* he saw the colt.

The aorist participle describes an action not related to the subject or object of the main clause e.g., loosing the ass, vengeance came. Note Vengeance did not loose he ass. To show this, both ass and loosing would be put in the GENITIVE case. Hence the construction is called the Genitive Absolute construction, but as the genitive and the ablative have the same form, it could also be called as in Latin the Ablative absolute construction.

13. Accusative and Infinitive

After verbs of saying, thinking, wishing (I Corin. 14:5), knowing perceiving, etc. Which take an indirect object, the Greek changes the expression e.g., "They believed that Socrates was a good man." This is called the Accusative and the infinitive construction.

This is not the only way of expressing the indirect statement, but it is unusual in English, though not unknown e.g., I saw him come i.e. I saw him (acc.) to come (inf.)

14. Negatives

Two negatives do not cancel out as in English, they are used for emphasis. e.g.

καὶ τὸν ἐρχόμενον πρὸς ἐμὲ οὐ μὴ ἐκβάλω ἔξω (and him who comes to me I shall by no means cast out). N. B. The extra emphasis in the Greek, NOT NOT, OUT OUT.

ου in a question expects the answer Yes. μη in a question expects the answer NO.

Translate the following:

Luke 23:37, 28 I Cor. 12:29, Gal. 3:20, 1 Cor. 3:3, Luke 20:45 (Ablative Absolute) With all the people hearing i.e. while all the people were hearing....

1 Cor. 3:1, 17.17. Note the not is equivalent to surely here, it expects the answer 'Yes!'

Start translating the Gospel and Epistle of John.

Appendix A

This book is based on the assumption, that a Greek Analytical Lexicon is used to assist the student in identifying the stem, and also to supplement the additional Paradigms or Patterns of certain Tense and Case Forms. Since this may not always be available. The following are added for ease of reference:

IMPORTANT FORMS OF THE VERB 'TO BE' (εἰμι)

Pres. Act. Indic. of εἰμι,		
	Singular	Plural
1.	εἰμί	ἐσμέν
2.	εἶ	ἐστέ
3.	ἐστί(ν)	εἰσί(ν)

Imper. Act. Indic. of εἰμι,		
	Singular	Plural
1.	ἤμην	ἦμεν
2.	ἦς	ἦτε
3.	ἦν	ἦσαν

Future Act. Indic. of εἰμι,		
	Singular	Plural
1.	ἔσομαι	ἐσόμεθα

Appendix A

2.	ἔσῃ	ἔσεσθε
3.	ἔσται	ἔσονται

Pres. Act. Subj. of εἰμί,		
	Singular	Plural
1.	ὦ	ὦμεν
2.	ᾖς	ἦτε
3.	ᾖ	ὦσι(ν)

Pres. Act. Imper. of εἰμί,		
	Singular	Plural
2.	ἴσθι	ἔστε
3.	ἔστω	ἔστωσαν

Present Participle of εἰμί ὤν, οὖσα, ὄν, being			
	Singular		
	M.	F.	N.
N.	ὤν	οὖσα	ὄν
G.	ὄντος	οὔσης	ὄντος
D.	ὄντι	οὔσῃ	ὄντι
A.	ὄντα	οὖσαν	ὄν
	Plural		
	M.	F.	N.
N.	ὄντες	οὖσαι	ὄντα
G.	ὄντων	οὐσῶν	ὄντων
D.	οὖσι(ν)	οὔσαις	οὖυσι(ν)
A.	ὄντας	οὔσας	ὄντα

Review—Differences in Expressing Greek and English

Important Pronouns

		Singular (this)	
	M.	F.	N.
N.	οὗτος	αὕτη	τοῦτο
G.	τούτου	ταύτης	τούτου
D.	τούτῳ	ταύτῃ	τούτῳ
A.	τοῦτον	ταύτην	τοῦτο

		Plural	
	M.	F.	N.
N.	οὗτοι	αὗται	ταῦτα
G.	τούτων	τούτων	τούτων
D.	τούτοις	ταύταις	τούτοις
A.	τούτους	ταύτας	ταῦτα

		Singular (that)	
	M.	F.	N.
N.	ἐκεῖνος	ἐκείνη	ἐκεῖνο
G.	ἐκείνου	ἐκείνης	ἐκείνου
D.	ἐκείνῳ	ἐκείνῃ	ἐκείνῳ
A.	ἐκεῖνον	ἐκείνην	ἐκεῖνο

		Plural	
	M.	F.	N.
N.	ἐκεῖνοι	ἐκεῖναι	ἐκεῖνα
G.	ἐκείνων	ἐκείνων	ἐκείνων
D.	ἐκείνοις	ἐκείναις	ἐκείνοις
A.	ἐκείνους	ἐκείνας	ἐκεῖνα

Appendix A

The personal pronouns I and you are used for emphasis. Below are given their forms.

(I)

	Singular	Plural
N.	ἐγώ	ἡμεῖς
G.	ἐμοῦ (μου)	ἡμῶν
D.	ἐμοί (μοι)	ἡμῖν
A.	ἐμέ (με)	ἡμᾶς

(you)		
	Singular	Plural
N.	σύ	ὑμεῖς
G.	σοῦ	ὑμῶν
D.	σοί	ὑμῖν
A.	σέ	ὑμᾶς

Sg. I, me, my to me are respectively: εγω με (or εμε) μου (or εμου)

Pl. We, us, our, to us are in order: ημεις ημας ημων ημιν You singular and plural in order are: συ σε σου σοι υμεις

Note the difference between you pl. beginning with υ, and we beginning with η.

Appendix B

IRREGULAR VERB FORMS FOUND IN JOHN CHAPTER 1 AND THEIR DERIVATIVES

Form	Derivative
ἦν	ειμι
ἐγένετο, γέγονεν	γινομαι
κατέλαβεν	καταλαμβανω
ἀπεσταλμένος	αποστελλω
ἦλθεν	ερχομαι
ἔγνω	γινωσκω
ἔλαβον	λαμβανω
ἔδωκεν, ἐδόθη	διδωμαι
γενέσθαι	γινομαι

Appendix B

κέκραγεν	κραζω
εἰπὸν	λεγω
ἑώρακεν	ὁραω
ἐξηγήσατο	εξηγεομαι
ἀπεκρίθη	αποκρινομαι
εἱστήκει	ἵστημι
κληθήσῃ	καλεω
ἀνεῳγότα	ανοιγω

THE MEANINGS CAN NOW B CHECKED IN ANY GREEK LEXICON FROM THE DERIVATIVES.

Other irregular verbs are listed in the more advanced grammars which we need for further mastery of New Testament Greek.

Read daily from your New Testament in Greek, and you will be surprised how soon you will be able to translate at speed.

Appendix C

TABLE OF THE REGULAR VERB

Principal part of λύω (stem λυ)

First Principal Part:

Indic	S	1	λύω	ἔλυον	λύομαι	ἐλυόμην
		2	λύεις	ἔλυες	λύῃ	ἐλύου
		3	λύει	ἔλυε(ν)	λύεται	ἐλύετο
	P	1	λύομεν	ἐλύομεν	λυόμεθα	ἐλυόμεθα
		2	λύετε	ἐλύετε	λύεσθε	ἐλύεσθε
		3	λύουσι(ν)	ἔλυον	λύονται	ἐλύοντο
Subj	S	1	λύω		λύωμαι	
		2	λύῃς		λύῃ	
		3	λύῃ		λύηται	
	P	1	λύωμεν		λυώμεθα	
		2	λύητε		λύησθε	
		3	λύωσι(ν)		λύωνται	

Appendix C

Opt	S	1	λύοιμι		λυοίμην	
		2	λύοις		λύοιο	
		3	λύοι		λύοιτο	
	P	1	λύοιμεν		λυοίμεθα	
		2	λύοιτε		λύοισθε	
		3	λύοιεν		λύοιντο	
Imptv	S	2	λῦε		λύου	
		3	λυέτω		λυέσθω	
	P	2	λύετε		λύεσθε	
		3	λυέτωσαν		λυέσθωσαν	
Inf			λύειν		λύεσθαι	
Part			λύων		λυόμενος	
			λύουσα		λυομένη	
			λῦον		λυόμενον	

Second Principal Part: λύσω

				Fut.Act.	Fut.Mid.	
Indic	S	1		λύσω	λύσομαι	
		2		λύσεις	λύσῃ	
		3		λύσει	λύσεται	
	P	1		λύσομεν	λυσόμεθα	
		2		λύσετε	λύσεσθε	
		3		λύσουσι(ν)	λύσονται	
Opt	S	1		λύσοιμι	λυσοίμην	
		2		λύσοις	λύσοιο	
		3		λύσοι	λύσοιτο	
	P	1		λύσοιμεν	λυσοίμεθα	
		2		λύσοιτε	λύσοισθε	

Table of the Regular Verb

		3	λύσοιεν	λύσοιντο
Inf			λύσειν	λύσεσθαι
Part			λύσων	λυσόμενος
			λύσουσα	λυσομένη
			λῦσον	λυσόμενον

Third Principal Part: ἔλυσα

			Aor.Act.	Aor.Mid.
Indic	S	1	ἔλυσα	ἐλυσάμην
		2	ἔλυσας	ἐλύσω
		3	ἔλυσε(ν)	ἐλύσατο
	P	1	ἐλύσαμεν	ἐλυσάμεθα
		2	ἐλύσατε	ἐλύσασθε
		3	ἔλυσαν	ἐλύσαντο
Subj	S	1	λύσω	λύσωμαι
		2	λύσῃς	λύσῃ
		3	λύσῃ	λύσηται
	P	1	λύσωμεν	λυσώμεθα
		2	λύσητε	λύσησθε
		3	λύσωσι(ν)	λύσωνται
Opt	S	1	λύσαιμι	λυσαίμην
		2	λύσαις	λύσαιο
		3	λύσαι	λύσαιτο
	P	1	λύσαιμεν	λυσαίμεθα
		2	λύσαιτε	λύσαισθε
		3	λύσαιεν	λύσαιντο
Imptv	S	2	λῦσον	λῦσαι
		3	λυσάτω	λυσάσθω

Appendix C

	P	2	λύσατε	λύσασθε
		3	λυσάτωσαν	λυσάσθωσαν
Inf			λῦσαι	λύσασθαι
Part			λύσας	λυσάμενος
			λύσασα	λυσαμένη
			λῦσαν	λυσάμενον

Fourth Principal Part: λέλυκα

			Perf.Act.	Plup.Act.
Indic	S	1	λέλυκα	(ἐ)λελύκειν
		2	λέλυκας	(ἐ)λελύκεις
		3	λέλυκε(ν)	(ἐ)λελύκει
	P	1	λελύκαμεν	(ἐ)λελύκειμεν
		2	λελύκατε	(ἐ)λελύκειτε
		3	λελύκασι(ν)	(ἐ)λελύκεισαν
			λέλυκαν	
Subj	S	1	λελύκω	
		2	λελύκῃς	
		3	λελύκῃ	
	P	1	λελύκωμεν	
		2	λελύκητε	
		3	λελύκωσι	
Opt	S	1	λελύκοιμι	
		2	λελύκοις	
		3	λελύκοι	
	P	1	λελύκοιμεν	
		2	λελύκοιτε	
		3	λελύκοιεν	

Table of the Regular Verb

Imptv	S	2	λέλυκε	
		3	λελυκέτω	
	P	2	λελύκετε	
		3	λελυκέτωσαν	
Inf			λελυκέναι	
Part			λελυκώς	
			λελυκυῖα	
			λελυκός	

Fifth Principal Part: λέλυμαι

			Plup.M.P.	Plup.M.P
Indic	S	2	λέλυμαι	ἐλελύμην
		3	λέλυσαι	ἐλέλυσο
	P	2	λέλυται	ἐλέλυτο
		3	λελύμεθα	ἐλελύμεθα
			λέλυσθε	ἐλέλυσθε
			λέλυνται	ἐλέλυντο
Imptv	S	2	λέλυσο	
		3	λελύσθω	
	P	2	λέλυσθε	
		3	λελύσθωσαν	
Inf			λελύσθαι	
Part			λελυμένος	
			λελυμένη	
			λελυμένον	

Appendix C

Sixth Principal Part: ἐλύθην

			Aor.Pass.	Fut.Pass
Indic	S	1	ἐλύθην	λυθήσομαι
		2	ἐλύθης	λυθήσῃ
		3	ἐλύθη	λυθήσεται
	P	1	ἐλύθημεν	λυθησόμεθα
		2	ἐλύθητε	λυθήσεσθε
		3	ἐλύθησαν	λυθήσονται
Subj	S	1	λυθῶ	
		2	λυθῇς	
		3	λυθῇ	
	P	1	λυθῶμεν	
		2	λυθῆτε	
		3	λυθῶσι(ν)	
Opt	S	1	λυθείην	λυθησοίμην
		2	λυθείης	λυθήσοιο
		3	λυθείη	λυθήσοιτο
	P	1	λυθείημεν	λυθησοίμεθα
		2	λυθείητε	λυθήσοισθε
		3	λυθείησαν	λυθήσοιντο
Imptv	S	2	λύθητι	
		3	λυθήτω	
	P	2	λύθητε	
		3	λυθήτωσαν	
Inf			λυθῆναι	λυθήσεσθαι
Part			λυθείς	λυθησόμενος
			λυθεῖσα	λυθησομένη
			λυθέν	λυθησόμενον

Excursus A[1]

A SYNTACTIC-ANALYTIC NEW TESTAMENT GREEK STUDY WITH A NEW PEDAGOGICAL CONSIDERATION

PEDAGOGICAL CONSIDERATION OF TEACHING NEW TESTAMENT GREEK

New Testament Greek is often a compulsory pre-requisite course in theological seminary education. However, it appears that it has become a heavy burden to most students who take the course. Many have to spend much time to learn to read the language. Unfortunately, not too many maintain their Greek after graduation. We, teachers of the New Testament Greek, are witnessing this problem with much pain. What has gone wrong?

Is it due to the fact that we do not have good tools, particularly from the pedagogical point of view? This paper develops the

1. By Dr. Sang-Hoon Kim, an Assistant Professor of NT, Chongshin Theological Seminary, South Korea.

Excursus A

thought that applied syntactic-semantic study can be of help in some measure in alleviating the difficulty. It draws upon scholars such as Johannes Louw, Douglas Stuart, Walter Kaiser, Gordon Fee, William Mounce, who have already been significant authorities and contributors in the area. However, any new pedagogical method needs to be carefully evaluated and revised for maximum effectiveness.

Modern Linguistics and Hermeneutics

Over the years, linguistics and hermeneutics have influenced each other and have been mutually beneficial. Right from the beginning[2] they have been inseparable. New and useful insights from linguistics have been reflected in the hermeneutics field. As linguists have developed their theories and obtained insights from the models of language or the data of linguistic phenomena, hermeneutics scholars have evaluated and applied their results in the interpretation of the Bible.

Modern linguistics, especially of the 20th century, placed much emphasis on the synchronic aspect of language, compared to the previous centuries in which the linguistics had been primarily concerned with the diachronic aspect. Most linguistic schools in the last century accepted synchronic priority as their approach.

The traditional grammatical-historical method has also shifted emphasis from the diachronic approach to the synchronic in interpretation. James Barr in 1961, Johannes Louw in 1973, and Moises Silva in 1983 have initiated and applied this synchronic approach to biblical interpretation.[3]

Discourse analysis (DA), a term first employed by Zellig Harris in 1952,[4] has gradually influenced the field of biblical in-

---

2. Cf. Stanly E. Porter, "In Defence of Verbal Aspect," 27–31; David Alan Black, *Linguistics and New Testament Interpretation*, 10.

3. James Barr, *The Semantics of Biblical Language*; Johannes P. Louw, "Discourse Analysis and the Greek New Testament"; Moises Silva, *Biblical Words and Their Meaning*.

4. DA was intended from the start not only to treat passages of written

terpretation. Black states[5] that the primary concern of DA is "to show the internal coherence or unity of a particular text." This is essentially the position of Louw, Nida, Porter, and Black. A reason why attention is paid to DA in biblical interpretation is that DA has extended the linguistic concerns to the larger units beyond a sentence.

In this endeavour the Chomskyan linguistic models (sentence-oriented), syntax and semantics, are combined with other insights (beyond the sentence level) into the interpretive process, appearing as various types of syntactic arrangements of the text.

The employment of these types of arrangement can be seen in the works of such scholars as Fee, Mounce, and Guthrie[6] in New Testament Greek.

These methods differ from the traditional way of interpretation, the grammatical-historical method, in terms of how to approach the text. The text is arranged for the purpose of visualization, letting the reader see the text with much clarity in terms of the grammatical function of each phrase and its connections. The visualized arrangement itself is applied from the area of syntax and semantics in modern linguistics.

Some strong points of this approach are as follows: (1) the relationships among the constituents of the sentence, such as "the main clause and sub-clause," "the subject-the predicative," et cetera, are clarified in diagram form, so that the interpreter can get a much clearer picture of the meaning; (2) the proper understanding of the syntactic structure of the text is displayed, and the connection between the main ideas and the subordinates is much clearly seen; (3) the syntactic structure of the text is more easily utilized in creating an expositional sermon or Group Bible Study outline.

---

language longer than the single sentence but also to relate language to behaviors and situations, to the extra-linguistic context.

5. Black, *Linguistics*, 12.

6. Gordon D. Fee, *New Testament Exegesis*; William D. Mounce, *A Graded Reader of Biblical Greek*; George H. Guthrie and J. Scott Duvall, *Biblical Greek Exegesis*.

Excursus A

Arrangements of the N. T. Greek Text?

Arrangement itself is an interpretive act, requiring an interpretive mind to treat the text properly. We may categorize the five ways of arrangement of the text according to their distinctive styles.

First, there is a traditional way, that is, verse by verse. Second, we can divide the text by segment and arrange it in the way of sequential order, based on the verse-division, such as 18a, 18b, 18c, 19a, 19b, 19c, and so on. This kind of division and arrangement can be seen in most exegeses or commentaries. Third, there is a way of just lining up sentences and numbering them, such as 1, 2, 3, 4, etc. Literary critics often use this method because literary texts, like novels or poems, do not normally present the verse division.

The aforementioned methods of arrangement are easy to follow, but they all lack an explicit display of the syntactic structure of the text and the relations among the syntactic components in the text, such as words, phrases, and sentences.

Fourth, there is a so-called colon arrangement, which was developed in South Africa.[7] Here, 'colon' refers to what the ancient Greek grammarians spoke of as a kind of thought unit. Although colon structure is essentially regarded as syntactic (because syntax and semantics cannot be easily separated), the pragmatic aim of colon analysis is to provide a satisfactory basis for a semantic interpretation of a text.

Fifth, there is a syntactical division and arrangement, the so-called "diagramming." It is designed to help the analyzer to visualize the syntactic structure of the text, the relations between phrases and clauses, and the basic flow of the argument through the text.[8] We can see this type of arrangement in Mounce,[9] Fee,[10]

---

7. Since Louw's article "Discourse Analysis and the Greek New Testament," *The Bible Translator* 24 (1973), 108–118.

8. Mounce, xv.

9. Mounce, *A Graded Reader of Biblical Greek*.

10. Fee, *New Testament Exegesis*.

A Syntactic-Analytic New Testament Greek Study

and Cotterell and Turner.[11] It is very helpful in the sense that it clarifies the syntactical relationships of the various words and word groups and makes it easier to discover the schematic flow of thoughts, whether in sentence or paragraph.[12] Its basic approach is to segment a passage into its phrases, particularly in consideration of clauses.

According to Mounce,[13] the syntactic diagram can help the reader to separate "the main ideas from the secondary" and to see "parallel thoughts," thus identifying the relationships among the phrases. He says, "in my experience of teaching intermediate Greek, next to developing a facility in the language, phrasing is the most significant tool my students learned."

Guthrie and Duvall[14] indicate certain strong points of this approach as follows: (1) the interest that can be extended into the realm of the Greek study; (2) the easiness to understand the larger units of the text, by effectively analyzing them; (3) the holistic approach in terms of integration between the study of Greek and applying the NT message, particularly in the exegetical process.

The advantage of "diagramming" is that "it forces one to identify grammatically every word in the passage,"[15] helping the reader to visualize the structures of the sentences and the flow of their logical argument. With this, the reader may confidently recognize the hierarchy of units in the text by determining integrated and complex sets of dependent relations.

There are certain sorts of rules that subdivide the sentences into phrases, although it seems to be difficult for the interpreter to keep the rules precise and consistent.[16]

11. Peter Cotterell and Max Turner, *Linguistics and Biblical Interpretation* (Illinois: InterVarsity Press, 1989).

12. The most proper unit for the explanation of the semantic content of the text is the paragraph that demonstrates the same semantic elements of coherence. See Louw, *Semantics*, 98, 116.

13. Mounce, *A Graded Reader*, xv.

14. George H. Guthrie and J. Scott Duvall, *Biblical Greek Exegesis*, 12–13.

15. Fee, *Exegesis*, 39.

16. Mounce advises us, "Lay out the phrases in a way that makes sense to you and shows you their structure, and do not worry if you are doing it 'right.'"

Excursus A

THE RULES OF THE SYNTACTIC-ANALYTIC ARRANGEMENTS

1. The syntactical order, in general, of the grammatical function in the sentence is as follows:

> The Subject
>   The Predicative
> The Objective
>   (or The Complement)
>   The Prepositional Phrase

The subject is first located to the left, and the predicate is next (indented, placed under it).

2. The syntactical order of the phrases (the main clause and its subordinate/s) is as follows:

> The Noun of The Subject (N)
>   N's modifier
>   The Predicative Verb (V)
>   V's adverbial phrase
>   The Objective (O)
>   O's modifier
>   The Complement (C)
>   C's modifier
>   The Prepositional Phrase (P)
>   P's modifier

The noun phrase (the nominative case) in the subject is furthest to the left. The main verb is placed next to the noun phrase or the subject.

3. The main clause is to the left, while the sub-clause is indented, one tap further than the main clause.

> The Main Clause
> ($N_1 + V_1$)
>   The Sub-Clause
>   ($N_2 + V_2$)

Cf. Mounce, *A Graded Reader*, xxiii.

4. Parallel phrases in apposition are indented the same distance from the left.

```
The Noun of The Subject (N)
    N's modifier 1
N's modifier 2
        The Predicative Verb (V)
            V's adverbial phrase
        The Objective (O)
            O's modifier 1
            O's modifier 2
```

5. The core noun of the subject and the predicate verb, whether they are in the main clause or in the sub-clause, are underlined and bold-typed.

```
[Main Clause]
            The Noun of The Subject (N)
                    The Predicative Verb (V)
    [Sub-Clause]
                    The Noun of The Subject (N)
                            The Predicative Verb (V)
```

6. A phrase can be subdivided into a smaller unit, as long as the phrase keeps its grammatical function. Thus, the modifier needs to be distinguished, by indentation, from the phrase that is modified or dominant.

```
The Noun of The Subject (N)
    N's modifier
        Modifier of the previous modifier
            Modifier of the next previous modifier
    The Predicative Verb (V)
        V's adverbial phrase
```

7. The connectives, whether coordinating or subordinating, are not left alone but rather stay with the following phrase.

Excursus A

> [Main Clause]
>   Connective 1 + <u>The Noun of The Subject (N)</u>
>   <u>The Predicative Verb (V)</u>
> [Sub-Clause]
>   Connective 2 + <u>The Noun of The Subject (N)</u>
>   <u>The Predicative Verb (V)</u>

COMPARISON OF VARIOUS TYPES OF ARRANGEMENT

There are various types of syntactic arrangements of the Greek text. Each pattern has its own principles and rules to be arranged in certain ways. We will compare those models of syntactic arrangements to my model, the Kim's diagram.

Comparison of the Leedy's (BibleWorks) Diagram and the Kim's, Ephesians 5:28a.

Leedy

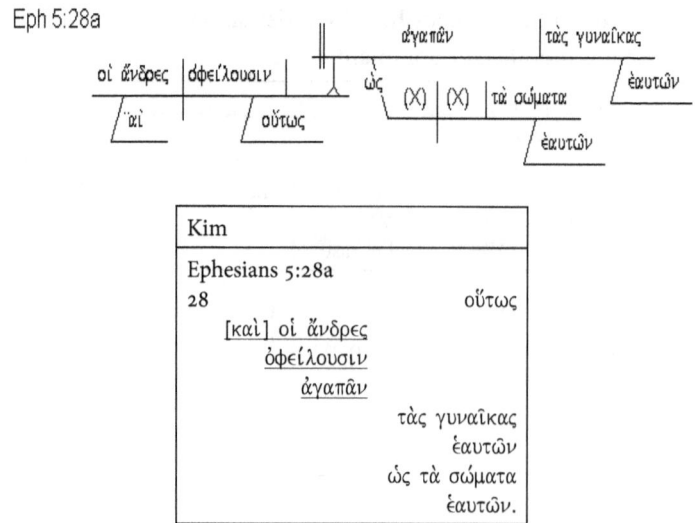

A Syntactic-Analytic New Testament Greek Study

The diagram newly appearing in BibleWorks 7.0 (Leedy's) is a traditional way, probably in the English world, of drawing the grammatical syntax in the sentence, intending to show the relationship among the words as precisely as possible.[17] As seen in Bible Works (Leedy's), the diagram demonstrates clearly the grammatical function of each word and its relationship at every level.

The problem is that its method is too complicated for the general user, who knows hardly the concept of the diagram to use it without sufficient training. In contrast to the former, the Kim's diagram looks simpler, showing the syntactic flow through the sentence, phrase by phrase. There are no grammatical signs. Thus, readers may make easy use of the method, drawing the diagram by themselves, once they get a few tips of arrangement of biblical Greek.

Comparison of the Fee's Model and the Kim's, 1 Thessalonians 1:2-3

	Fee[A]
2	Εὐχαριστοῦμεν τῷ θεῷ
	πάντοτε
	περὶ πάντων ὑμῶν
	ποιούμενοι μνείαν
	ἀδιαλείπτως
	ἐπὶ τῶν προσευχῶν ἡμῶν,
3	μνημονεύοντες ὑμῶν τοῦ ἔργου
	τῆς πίστεως
	καὶ τοῦ κόπου
	τῆς ἀγάπης
	καὶ τῆς ὑπομονῆς
	τῆς ἐλπίδος
	τοῦ κυρίου ἡμῶν
	Ἰησοῦ
	Χριστοῦ
	ἔμπροσθεν τοῦ θεοῦ καὶ πατρὸς ἡμῶν,
A. Fee, *New Testament Exegesis*, 76.	

---

17. We can see this type of model in the book by Curtis Vaughan and Virtus E. Gideon, *A Greek Grammar of the New Testament: A Workbook Approach to Intermediate Grammar* (Nashville: Broadman Press, 1979).

Excursus A

Kim

2   Εὐχαριστοῦμεν
        τῷ θεῷ
            πάντοτε
            περὶ πάντων ὑμῶν
        ποιούμενοι
            μνείαν
                ἐπὶ τῶν προσευχῶν
                  ἡμῶν,
              ἀδιαλείπτως
3   μνημονεύοντες
            ὑμῶν
            τοῦ ἔργου
              τῆς πίστεως
            καὶ τοῦ κόπου
              τῆς ἀγάπης
            καὶ τῆς ὑπομονῆς
              τῆς ἐλπίδος
                τοῦ κυρίου
                  ἡμῶν
                Ἰησοῦ Χριστοῦ
              ἔμπροσθεν τοῦ θεοῦ
                  καὶ πατρὸς
                    ἡμῶν,

The Kim's diagram is very similar to Fee's model, particularly in the style of phrasal subdivision. However, the two models show some differences from each other.

One of the peculiarities of the Kim's model is that phrasal subdivision is relatively shorter than the Fee's. The rule of division is probably clearer, phrase by phrase, just one step further indented, placed under the previous phrase. By this, the grammatical function of each phrase can be simply demonstrated.

The location of the subject that is first placed to the left is empty in the Kim's chart above, for the subject is omitted and is included in the predicative verb. The two models differ in that the prepositional phrases in the latter are indented and located one step further after the object or the complement, as in v.3.

A Syntactic-Analytic New Testament Greek Study

Comparison of the Mounce's Model and the Kim's, 1 John 1:3

Mounce[A]

3 ὃ ἑωράκαμεν
καὶ
ἀκηκόαμεν,
ἀπαγγέλλομεν καὶ ὑμῖν,
ἵνα καὶ ὑμεῖς κοινωνίαν ἔχητε
                                        μεθ' ἡμῶν.
καὶ … δὲ
ἡ κοινωνία … ἡ ἡμετέρα
    μετὰ   τοῦ πατρὸς
    καὶ
    μετὰ   τοῦ υἱοῦ αὐτοῦ
                       Ἰησοῦ Χριστοῦ.

A. Mounce, *A Graded Reader*, 10.

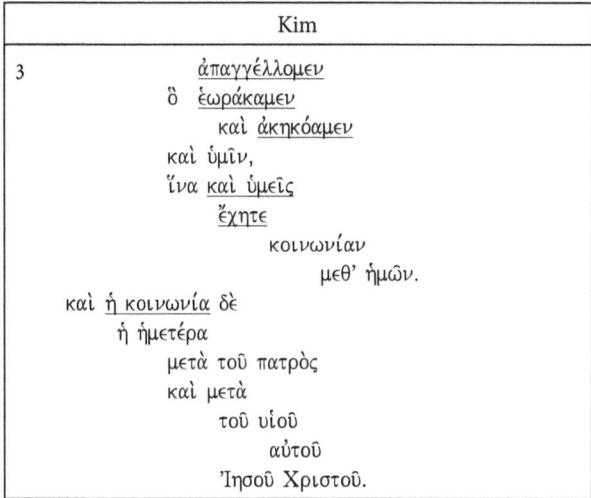

Kim

3   ἀπαγγέλλομεν
   ὃ ἑωράκαμεν
      καὶ ἀκηκόαμεν
   καὶ ὑμῖν,
   ἵνα καὶ ὑμεῖς
       ἔχητε
          κοινωνίαν
            μεθ' ἡμῶν.
καὶ ἡ κοινωνία δὲ
ἡ ἡμετέρα
   μετὰ τοῦ πατρὸς
   καὶ μετὰ
      τοῦ υἱοῦ
      αὐτοῦ
      Ἰησοῦ Χριστοῦ.

There is no major difference between the two models above. However, key differences between the Mounce's phrasing model and the Kim's diagram can be stated as follows: (1) the latter has more specific subdivision on each phrase; (2) the location of the subject and predicative differs from each other; (3) the connectives such

Excursus A

and καί and δέ are differently arranged; (4) even the sub-clause, such as the ἵνα clause, is subdivided as exactly the same as the main clause is done in the Kim's; (5) the subordinates are consistently indented, i.e., placed under the phrases to which they are related.

Comparison of the Guthrie-Duvall's Model and the Kim's, Colossians 3:1-2

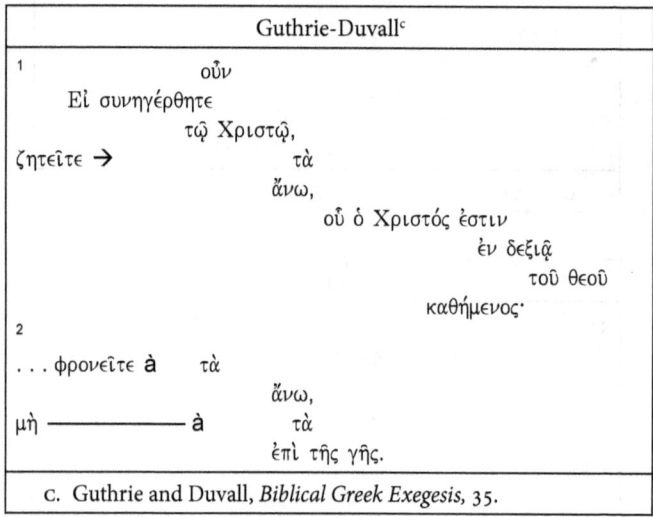

c. Guthrie and Duvall, *Biblical Greek Exegesis*, 35.

A Syntactic-Analytic New Testament Greek Study

	Kim

1	Εἰ οὖν <u>συνηγέρθητε</u>
	    τῷ Χριστῷ,
	  <u>ζητεῖτε</u>
	    τὰ ἄνω,
	      οὗ <u>ὁ Χριστός</u>
	        <u>ἐστιν</u>
	          καθήμενος
	            ἐν δεξιᾷ
	              τοῦ θεοῦ·

2	<u>φρονεῖτε</u>
	    τὰ ἄνω,
	    μὴ τὰ ἐπὶ τῆς γῆς.

The strength of Guthrie-Duvall is that it shows the grammatical function of the phrases, explicitly regarding the verbal phrases. But Kim's does not use any grammatical signs, for it considers them unnecessary. The connection between the predicative verb and the object is clear, as long as the two are located where they should be, according to the rules of arrangements.

The Kim's diagram looks very compact but also coherent in its structure, being easily and simply organized.

Questionnaire Responses

For the purposes of this paper, I posed several questions to my students, regarding their experience in using the syntactic-analytic arrangement of the Greek Bible (from now on SABG) and their practical uses of both the method and its materials.

239 students participated, most of whom have been trained very recently for around two months. They are all M. Div. students including 14 students of the M. Div. equivalent.

1. About their biblical Greek abilities

Excursus A

Among 239 students, 17.6% replied that they can read and understand biblical Greek (from now on BG), if some helps, such as Greek dictionaries and Bible Software (like BibleWorks), are available for them. 31.8% thought that they are at the level of just finishing the basic grammar of BG. 50.6% of students confessed that they could not remember even the basic grammar.[18]

2. About relationship between SABG and learning of BG

27.6% replied that the Greek study by means of SABG was most helpful for them to learn BG and to get better a understanding of BG, and 55.2% answered that they got some benefits (partially) from SABG, while 17.2% responded negatively to the question. Probably among the negative responders, some of them might have not yet understood the relationship between the two. The others do not yet have any benefit from the method (SABG), because they have not yet had enough time to learn and practice the method.

The students who have studied SABG over six months (up to 11 months) replied quite positively. 68.7% said that they were helped very much in learning BG, while 31.3% replied that they had some benefits from it.

As these students study SABG, they recognize that they are improving gradually in learning BG. As long as they experience and practice SABG, they get familiar with BG more and more.

3. About the relationship between SABG and the interpretation of the text

70.7% responded to the question that it becomes much easier for them to interpret the Greek text, while 5.4% felt just a little bit easier than before, and 23.9% thought that SABG is still complicated for them in using it to read the text. All the students who have experienced SABG over the six months (100%) felt so much easier to grasp the meaning of the text than in the past.

18. Such passive attitude is probably due to the fact that they did not have any chance, unfortunately, to continue to learn the Greek during the last semester.

These statistics indicate that many students who have experienced SABG have practical benefits in interpreting the biblical text.

    4. About the relationship between SABG and understanding of the logic (or logicality) of the sentence.

56.1% replied that SABG helped them much to understand the logic of the sentence, while 41.0% said that it did only partly, and 2.9% was negative.

87.5% of those who studied over six months responded that they could understand well the logic of the sentence by means of SABG, while just 12.5% got only some benefits from SABG.

If the students understand the logical structure of the sentence(s), it means, they can clearly grasp the coherent meaning in the biblical text. Thus, they will improve in doing interpretation as much as they can find out the logic of the author. For this, SABG is useful.

    5. About their understanding of the rules of SABG

7.9% thought that they fully understood the rules of SABG, how to syntactically arrange the Greek text, while 71.6% believe that they understood it to some extent, and 20.5% hardly understood how to arrange the text in the SABG way.

There are two small classes that I have been teaching regarding how to understand and utilize SABG for preparing the expositional sermons, two hours every week since September 2006. In the first class, 20.0% replied that they understood the rules, while 76.0% did to some extent, and 4.0% had difficulties to understand them at the moment. In the second class, their responses were 7.2%, 85.7%, and 7.1%, respectively.

    6. The extent to which they become more interested in BG or not, after they have been taught in the SABG way.

59.8% showed a positive response to the question that they became more interested in BG than before, while 40.2% admitted that they experienced no difference in their interest in BG after studying SABG for two months.

Excursus A

The students who were voluntarily involved in the SABG study group all positively responded as they got more interested in BG than before.

Around the 60% of the students demonstrated that they became more interested in BG after studying SABG. The SABG method seemed to have encouraged some of the students to keep themselves interested in BG and to use BG in their ministries, such as in preparation for sermons.

7. Whether they want to keep studying using SABG or not 59.8% replied that they would continue to study SABG, while 35.6% answered that they would study SABG, only when they needed it. 95.4% expressed their desire to study SABG for their own benefit. 4.6% were negative.

The more some of these students used SABG, the more they wanted to keep up the method. Among the class students who studied more seriously than others, 79.5% expressed their desire to keep up SABG, while 20.5% answered that they would use this method, only occasionally. There was no negative response in this group. All the volunteers who studied SABG responded that they would keep it up.

Overall, most of the respondents showed positive concerns about SABG, and if these practise on a regular basis, they will be more likely to utilise BG in their ministries and academic research.

8. About the interlinear subscripts of translation in Korean-English on each Greek phrase

61.9% indicated that the interlinear subscripts were so very useful for them to grasp the meaning of SABG, while 35.2% thought that they only got some benefits from these subscripts, and 2.9% thought that the interlinear subscripts were not necessary for them.

The interlinear subscripts are designed to help many students who are not very familiar with BG. We may say that it is working. For the students who rather get disturbed by the subscripts, SABG without subscripts can be available. As the students who first needed such subscripts get accustomed to SABG and improve in handling BG, they will no longer rely on such subscripts.

Four Characteristics of SABG

1. Simplicity

The diagram that simply subdivides each phrase in terms of grammatical sense can be created by the users, once they receive an orientation of just a few hours. There are no grammatical signs.

2. Practicality

Is it practical for the user to use it? Bible students can use this tool to prepare expositional sermons and Bible study questions. This method provides an excellent diagram that reveals the cohesive structure of the text clearly and neatly.

3. Flexibility

This tool can flexibly accommodate the various needs of the users. For the students who are trained in BG, the diagram can be used as arranged only in Greek, while for the students who are not comfortable with Greek, the diagram can be supplemented with the interlinear subscripts of translation, parsing, and basic forms of Greek vocabularies.

4. Availability

Although the method itself is useful, if the data are not sufficient, the method and its use are no use to students. For the availability of the method in the fullest degree the data on the entire text should be produced by the specialists as quickly as possible.[19]

---

19. I am steadily working on the entire Greek text to produce syntactically arranged data for the students and church ministers, which will consist of five volumes. I hope that the first book could be published by the end of next year. On the other hand, the syntactically arranged text of the Korean New Testament (only in Korean) has already been printed in two volumes. A revised syntactic arrangement of the Bible in Korean, including the Old Testament, will be published. Both projects are initiated by the author in South Korea.

Excursus A

The Problem is the Pedagogy

Most graduates of theological seminaries end up gradually losing their skills in biblical Greek. They spend a good amount of time reading theological books but do not continue to use biblical Greek after graduation. They just rely on English and Korean Bibles rather than the Greek one. Their costly effort of hard labour to learn Greek during their seminary days is wasted.

What is the problem? The problem may lie in the teaching-and-learning method, particularly in the pedagogical mechanism. How should we help students to effectively improve themselves in biblical Greek? How can we encourage them to keep up their interest in it, so that they continue to use Greek even after they graduate? How can we help the church ministers to use Greek for their varied ministries?

If they are convinced that they can satisfactorily obtain the useful data from their study of Greek, if they can gather practical results without spending too much time, and if they can have an easy access to well-designed diagrams of the biblical Greek text and use them to their fullest satisfaction, what difference would that make?

The pedagogical development of the Kim's syntactic-analytic arrangement of the Greek text is still in progress; it is presently been reconsidered, re-evaluated, readjusted, reapplied, and hopefully, effectively and usefully.

Excursus B

JOHN 1:1–18: BLOCK DIAGRAMMING OF JNT, NIV, GNT[1]

JNT

di Wod did de bout,
  wen taim did staat,
    an
di Wod did de de wid Gad.
    Matarafak,
di Wod a did Gad.
2 Di Wod did de bout wid Gad
  fram bifuo di worl kom bout.
3 Gad kaaz di wan we a di Wod fi mek evriting.
Notn no de we im neehn mek.

---

1. Jamaican New Testament, New International Version, Greek New Testament, respectively.

Excursus B

4Im a di wan we mek evriting liv,
                an
a im kyari lait
      kom gi piipl
      so dem kyan si.
5Im shain an lait op di daak
                An
di daak kudn tap di lait
                fram shain!
6   Nou
yu did av wan man
      we Gad did sen kom.
Im niem Jan.
7Gad did sen Jan
      fi tel piipl
            bout di wan we a di lait
      so dem kuda biliiv
            we Jan se.
8Jan a neehn di lait.
Im did onggl kom
      fi tel piipl
      bout di lait.
9Da lait de a di riil lait
    an
im kom iina di worl
    an
mek evribadi nuo im.
10A im mek di worl
    an
im kom liv iina it
    bot
di piipl dem neehn nuo a uu im.
      iina di worl

John 1:1–18: Block Diagramming of JNT, NIV, GNT

11 Im kom
      tu im uona konchri
      an
im uona piipl dem ton dem bak pan im.
12   Bot
az fi aal a dem we welkom im — dat fi se, dem we chos
      iina im an im niem,
im gi dem di rait
      fi ton Gad pikni.
13   bot
dem no baan iina Gad fambili laka ou naamal pikni baan
      wid mada an faada
          ar
kaaz sumadi did fiil fi av seks
          ar
kaaz wan ozban mek op im main se im waahn pikni.
Nuo! A Gad imself mek dem baan.
14   Nou,
di wan we a di Wod ton man,
im kom kom liv mongks wi,
      an
wi si ou im big an powaful.
Im a Faada Gad wan an onggl dege-dege Bwai Pikni.
Faada Gad sen im kom
      an
a di Faada mek im so big an powaful.
Di Bwai Pikni shuo wi nof nof lov iivn duo wi no dizorv it,
      an
a bier chuu sitn im shuo wi bout Gad.
15 Jan kom an im tel piipl bout im.
Im baal out an tel dem se,
"Da wan ya, a im mi did a taak bout wen mi tel unu se,
'Di sumadi we de kom afta mi, im wie wie biga an beta dan mi,

Excursus B

    kaaz im did de bout fram lang bifuo mi baan.'"
16 wi get muo lov fram im pan tap a di lov we wi did a get aredi
   sieka ou im lov wi so moch
     an
  tel wi bier chuu sitn
   bout Gad,
    17Kaaz, yu si, Gad gi Muoziz di Laa

            fi gi wi,
  bot
im yuuz Jiizas
 fi mek wi nuo wa chuu,
  an
im shuo wi lov
 we wi no dizorv
   sieka Jiizas,.
18Nobadi neva eva si Gad yet.
Di onggl sumadi we eva si im a di wan dege-dege Bwai Pikni,

          we a
         Gad imself.
Im wel kluos
 tu di Faada,
  an
a im mek wi nuo wa di Faada komiin laik.

John 1:1–18: Block Diagramming of JNT, NIV, GNT

NIV

The Word was
    in the beginning,
        and
the Word was
    with God,
        and
the Word was God.
² He was
    with God
    in the beginning.
³ all things were made
    through him;
nothing was made that has been made
    without him.
⁴ Life was
    in him
    and
that life was the light
        of all mankind.
⁵ The light shines
    in the darkness,
    and
the darkness has not overcome it.
⁶ There was a man
        whose name was John
        sent from God
⁷ He came as a witness
    to testify
        concerning that light,
    so that
    all might believe

Excursus B

        through him.
[8] He himself was not the light;
he came only as a witness
        to the light= the true light . . . coming into the world
            that gives light to everyone.
[9] . [10] He was in the world,
        and
the world did not recognize him
        though the world was made
            through him.
[11] He came to that which was his own,
        but
his own did not receive him.
[12]   Yet
he gave the right to become children of God
        to all who did receive him, to those who believed in his name,— [13] children born not of natural descent,
        nor of human decision
        or a husband's will,
        but born of God.
[14] The Word became flesh
        and
made his dwelling
        among us.
We have seen his glory, the glory of the one and only Son,
        who came
            from the Father,
        full of grace and truth.
[15] John testified
        concerning him.

John 1:1–18: Block Diagramming of JNT, NIV, GNT

He cried out,
    saying, "This is the one I spoke about
        when I said, 'He who comes after me has
   surpassed me
           because he was
               before me.'"
[16] We have all received grace
          in place of grace already given
          out of his fullness
[17]   For
the law was given
      through Moses;
grace and truth came
      through Jesus Christ.
[18] No one has ever seen God,
    but
the one and only Son has made him known
       who is himself God and is in closest relationship
       with the Father.

Excursus B

GNT

ὁ λόγος
    ἐν ἀρχῇ ἦν

    καὶ

ὁ λόγος ἦν πρὸς τὸν θεόν

    καὶ

ὁ λόγος ἦν θεὸς

[2] οὗτος ἦν ἐν ἀρχῇ

    πρὸς τὸν θεόν.

[3] πάντα ἐγένετο

    δι' αὐτοῦ

    καὶ

οὐδὲ ἕν ἐγένετο

    χωρὶς αὐτοῦ.

ὃ γέγονεν ἦν ζωὴ

[4]   ἐν αὐτῷ

    καὶ

John 1:1-18: Block Diagramming of JNT, NIV, GNT

ἡ ζωὴ ἦν τὸ φῶς

  τῶν ἀνθρώπων·

5   καὶ

τὸ φῶς φαίνει
  ἐν τῇ σκοτίᾳ

  καὶ

ἡ σκοτία αὐτὸ οὐ κατέλαβεν.

⁶ ἄνθρωπος Ἐγένετό
    ἀπεσταλμένος
      παρὰ θεοῦ
ὄνομα
αὐτῷ Ἰωάννης·
⁷ οὗτος ἦλθεν
    εἰς μαρτυρίαν
    ἵνα μαρτυρήσῃ
      περὶ τοῦ φωτός
      ἵνα πάντες πιστεύσωσιν
        δι' αὐτοῦ
⁸ ἐκεῖνος οὐκ ἦν τὸ φῶς
   ἀλλ'
   [ἐκεῖνος ἦλθεν]
    ἵνα μαρτυρήσῃ
      περὶ τοῦ φωτός
⁹ τὸ φῶς τὸ ἀληθινόν ἦν
   ὃ φωτίζει πάντα ἄνθρωπόν
   [ὃ] ἐρχόμενον εἰς τὸν κόσμον
¹⁰ ἦν

Excursus B

ἐν τῷ κόσμῳ
    καὶ
ὁ κόσμος ἐγένετό
    δι' αὐτοῦ
    καὶ
ὁ κόσμος οὐκ ἔγνω αὐτὸν
[11] ἦλθέν
    εἰς τὰ ἴδια
    καὶ
οἱ ἴδιοι οὐ παρέλαβον αὐτὸν
    δὲ
[12] ὅσοι ἔλαβον αὐτόν
ἔδωκεν ἐξουσίαν
    αὐτοῖς
    γενέσθαι τέκνα θεοῦ
    τοῖς πιστεύουσιν
    εἰς τὸ ὄνομα αὐτοῦ
[13] οἳ ἐγεννήθησαν
    οὐκ ἐξ αἱμάτων
    οὐδὲ ἐκ θελήματος σαρκὸς
    οὐδὲ ἐκ θελήματος ἀνδρὸς
    ἀλλ'
    ἐκ θεοῦ
[14]   καὶ
ὁ λόγος ἐγένετο σὰρξ
    καὶ
    ἐσκήνωσεν
        ἐν ἡμῖν
    καὶ
    ἐθεασάμεθα τὴν δόξαν αὐτοῦ
        δόξαν ὡς μονογενοῦς
            παρὰ πατρός

John 1:1-18: Block Diagramming of JNT, NIV, GNT

πλήρης χάριτος καὶ
ἀληθείας
¹⁵ Ἰωάννης μαρτυρεῖ
περὶ αὐτοῦ
καὶ
κέκραγεν
λέγων
οὗτος ἦν ὃν
εἶπον
ὁ ἐρχόμενος
ὀπίσω μου
γέγονεν᾿ ἔμπροσθέν μου
ὅτι
ἢν πρῶτός μου

¹⁶ ὅτι
ἡμεῖς πάντες ἐλάβομεν καὶ χάριν
ἀντὶ χάριτος
ἐκ τοῦ πληρώματος αὐτοῦ
¹⁷ ὅτι
ὁ νόμος ἐδόθη
διὰ Μωϋσέως
ἡ χάρις καὶ ἡ ἀλήθεια ἐγένετὸ
διὰ Ἰησοῦ Χριστοῦ
¹⁸ οὐδεὶς ἑώρακεν θεὸν
πώποτε·
μονογενὴς θεὸς= ἐκεῖνος ἐξηγήσατο
ὁ ὢν εἰς τὸν κόλπον τοῦ πατρὸς

Excursus B

ASSIGNMENT:

Diagram any seven (7) of the following sentences:

1. ἱλαρὸν γὰρ δότην ἀγαπᾷ ὁ θεός
2. ἀγαπᾷ γὰρ ἱλαρὸν δότην ὁ θεός
3. δότην γὰρ ἀγαπᾷ ἱλαρὸν ὁ θεός
4. ὁ θεός γὰρ ἀγαπᾷ ἱλαρὸν δότην
5. δότην γὰρ ὁ θεός ἀγαπᾷ ἱλαρὸν
6. ἀγαπᾷ γὰρ ἱλαρὸν δότην ὁ θεός
7. ἀγαπᾷ γὰρ ἱλαρὸν ὁ θεός δότην
8. δότην γὰρ ἀγαπᾷ ὁ θεός ἱλαρὸν
9. ἱλαρὸν γὰρ ἀγαπᾷ ὁ θεός δότην
10. ἱλαρὸν γὰρ δότην ὁ θεός ἀγαπᾷ
11. δότην γὰρ ὁ θεός ἀγαπᾷ ἱλαρὸν
12. ἱλαρὸν γὰρ ἀγαπᾷ ὁ θεός δότην
13. ἱλαρὸν γὰρ δότην ὁ θεός ἀγαπᾷ
14. ὁ θεός γὰρ δότην ἀγαπᾷ ἱλαρὸν

Now try your hand at:
οὕτως γὰρ ἠγάπησεν ὁ θεὸς τὸν κόσμον, ὥστε τὸν υἱὸν τὸν μονογενῆ ἔδωκεν, ἵνα πᾶς ὁ πιστεύων εἰς αὐτὸν μὴ ἀπόληται ἀλλ' ἔχῃ ζωὴν αἰώνιον.

Excursus Γ

THE LANGUAGE OF THE NEW TESTAMENT

If the language of Jesus was Semitic, Paul's was definitely Greek. His letters have come down to us in this language, and that of the Koine variety. At the time of the apostle it was the *lingua franca* of the Mediterranean world, legacy of the great Alexander of Macedonia; and while Jesus must have been fluent in Hebrew and especially Aramaic, Greek must have been known to him as well. Once thought to be a combination of the Classical and Hebrew by some scholars, we have come to realize that the language of Paul was indeed the language of the common wo/man. This knowledge has been vouch-safed through the discoveries of various papyrus materials in Egypt.

The Greek language in general has over 3000 years of history, from the 16th century BCE to the present. The Koine, the language of Paul, flourished between BCE 300–300 CE. In comparison to the forms which preceded it, the Koine was characterized by simplicity of syntax, form and vocabulary amenable and useful for merchants, travelers, soldiers and statesmen alike. This is well attested by the thousands of Papyri found in North Africa, preserving "for

Excursus Γ

us the actual life of the day and includ[ing] letters of all sorts . . . contracts, receipts, proclamations, anything, everything."[1]

Accepting the overall contribution of the masses of Greek papyri on our understanding of the NT, some feel, however, that their value has been overstated to the neglect of other important features, such the influence of the LXX and, what the REB calls, the Jewish languages. In other words, not all important terms in the Greek New Testament can be elucidated by invoking the papyri.

There are many words that are best understood against a Semitic background, and even where the papyri shed light on some terms, a more complete colouring can be seen from the perspective of the Aramaic or Hebrew.

So with this caveat in mind, there is a wealth of knowledge to be gained by carefully weighing the vocabulary of Paul in the light emanating from the ancient Orient.[2] Thus we read:

> St. Paul too can command the terse pithiness of the homely gospel speech, especially in his ethical exhortations as pastor. These take shape naturally in clear-cut *maxims* such as the people themselves use and treasure up. But even where St. Paul is arguing to himself and takes more to the language of the middle class, even where he is carried away by priestly fervour of the liturgist [cf. Rom. 15] and the enthusiasm of the psalmist [e.g., Rom. 3: 10–18], his Greek never becomes literary. . . . thickly studded with the rugged, forceful words taken from the popular idiom [like that of Rasta] , it is perhaps the most brilliant example of the artless though not inartistic colloquial prose of a traveled city resident of the Roman Empire, its wonderful flexibility making it just the Greek for use in a mission to all the world.

Since Deissmann wrote, not a few studies have demonstrated that the apostle was a much better literary artist than was first imagined. But what Deissmann and his followers have done is to put beyond doubt the character of Paul's writings as 'Holy Ghost'

---

1. Robertson and Davis, *Short Grammar*, 12–13.
2. Deissmann, *Light from the Ancient East* , 63–64.

The Language of the New Testament

language dressed in the garment of a Greco-Roman. But where the nominative 'I' is concerned there does not seem to be any great deal of difference between the Koine usage and its classical counterpart. The only possible exceptions to this are the Gospels, where the influence of Hebraism appears substantial. The few published examples from the papyri seem to support this: ἐγὼ νόμους ἀθρώπους ἐθέμην᾽ ... ἐγώ Κρόνου θυγάτηρ πρεσβυτάτη ... ἐγώ εἰμι ἡ ἀλήθεια ....[3] The lines, which predate the time of Jesus, remind one of certain Johannine passages, especially the words I have underscored.

More recent studies of the language of Paul's letters have returned to an emphasis which was that of early Greek grammarians, that is, on the verb. In fact, the modern study is enriched by the study of linguistics, particularly the investigation into the nature of the verbal system. Over two decades ago two scholars, namely, Fanning and Porter[4], published revisions of their doctoral work in the area of aspectual theory. The latter, for instance, defines verbal aspect as '*a semantic (meaning) category by which a speaker or writer grammaticalizes (i.e represents a meaning by choice of a word-form) a perspective on action by selection of a particular tense-form in the verbal system* (Porter italics his).[5]

This understanding of aspect, then, links the form of the verb (morphology) with its function. Although the concept of aspect is closely tied to the tense forms, Porter feels strongly that the verbs *qua* verbs have nothing to do with temporal matters. These can only be inferred from the context. For Porter, there are three verbal aspects that were available in Paul's day. This therefore means that in the writing of Romans, for example, one may very well find 1) the aspect complete in which '*the action is conceived of . . . as complete and undifferentiated process*' (e.g., Rom. 5:14), 2) the aspect continuous in which the language depicts an action in progress (Rom. 6:8), or 3) the aspect as complex, in which '*the state of action*

---

3. Moulton and Milligan, *The Vocabulary of the Greek Testament*, 180.
4. Fanning, *Verbal Aspect*.
5. Porter, *Verbal Aspect*.

109

Excursus Γ

is conceived of by the language user as reflecting a given . . . state of affairs'[6] (e.g., Rom. 6:7; Porter's italics).

Certain verbs, however, particularly εἰμί, found regularly on the lips of the Jesus of the Gospels, do not carry any aspectual feature whatever, and so as a consequence may have very little exegetical significance.[7] Of course, an affirmation like ἐγώ εἰμι ἡ ἀλήθεια (John 14: 6) or ἐγώ εἰμι σάρκινός (Rom. 7: 14) will have exegetical significance in their respective contexts that would be determined, not by the aspectually 'challenged' linking verb, but perhaps by the prominent nominative and the contextual force of the discourse.

> In essential agreement with Porter, at least at the level of definition, is Buist Fanning.[8] His conviction is that verbal aspect is too dependent on other features of the context for it *alone* [his emphasis] to be determinative in interpretation. However, [aspect] in combination with other features . . . is a significant linguistic element to be weighed in interpreting a number of texts in the NT. . . .[9]

Porter would agree with Fanning's distinction between *aktionsart*, an early twentieth century description of the fundamental function of the verb, and aspect. Whereas *aktionsart* is said to describe how an action actually occurs, aspect, on the other hand, 'involves a way of viewing the action; [it] reflects the subjective conception or portrayal by the speaker; focuses the speaker's representation of the action.'[10]

But despite their general agreement on the importance of the subject, Porter and Fanning, it has been observed, have some serious differences in the way they perceive how this promising

---

6. Ibid., 22.

7. Future tense verbs are also 'aspectually vague' Porter, *Aspect*, 23.

8. Later (p.1) he seems to cite approvingly those scholars who distinguish the tenses from aspect, which is 'concerned rather with features like duration, progression, completion, repetition, inception, current relevance and their opposites.

9. Fanning, *Aspect* ,vi.

10. Ibid., 31.

approach to the study of the Greek verbal system apply to the Pauline and other NT corpora. For instance, Porter believes that the high incidence of present subjunctives in 1 Thessalonians may have been chosen by the writer to express urgency, while Fanning gives a similar emphasis to corresponding aorists.

Since aspectology is such a young and complex discipline, and since its serious application to the NT has barely begun, it is definitely too early to determine its full contribution to the understanding of Paul's usage of language, particularly in the book of Romans. Notwithstanding this reality, the works of Porter or Fanning in this regard should be consulted for any light they may shed on even familiar passages.[11]

SUMMARY

The character of the Greek of Paul and the other NT writers may best be summarized in the words of a twentieth-century translator:

> I must, in common justice, confess here that for many years I had viewed the Greek of the New Testament with a rather snobbish disdain. I had read the best of Classical Greek both at school and Cambridge for over ten years. To come down to the *Koine* of the first century A.D. seemed, I have sometimes remarked rather uncharitably, like reading Shakespeare for some years and turning to the Vicar's letter in the Parish Magazine! But I think now that I was wrong: I can see that the expression of the Word of God in ordinary workaday language is all a piece with God's incredible humility in becoming Man in Jesus Christ. And, further, the language itself is not as pedestrian as I had at first supposed.[12]

---

11. After commenting on a methodological problem that may be responsible for differences between Fanning and Porter, Silva (*Biblical Words*, 81–82) advises pastors and exegetes to say very little about Aspect.

12. Phillips, *Ring of Truth*, 18.

Excursus Δ

15 REASONS WHY JAMAICAN PATOIS IS A LANGUAGE?

By Karl Folkes

In the fifteen points below I have summarized the issues on why Jamaican Patois is a language. As a Jamaican educator and linguist I have been working diligently to have our Jamaican language fully and officially recognized by our Jamaican Government. So far I've been receiving favorable commentary from the Jamaican Press and the Jamaican Government. Thanks for your highly valuable support! Karl Folkes (Yaadibwai).

Fifteen points on "why Jamaican Patois is a language":

1. Creole languages are in effect the modern languages of the world; and have evolved and developed with varying degrees of automaticity over the last 400 years.
2. There are more than 200 attested Creole languages in the world and represented in all continents of the globe.
3. Creole languages are popularly described as evolving from an earlier 'Pidgin,' or putatively "less fully-developed form."

15 Reasons why Jamaican Patois is a Language?

However, this is merely a linguistic theory framed within a Western European ideological worldview.

4. The majority of Creole languages (again, the term 'Creole' is of European origin, and therefore troublesome for several reasons) have their origins in African languages. Thus, while their vocabulary or lexicon may be largely European-based (with lexical contributions from the hypothesized 'superstrate' languages), their syntax or grammar is distinctly non-European, and certainly more closely African (a continent historically described as "the dark continent" and therefore genetically contributing hypothesized 'substrate' languages).

5. The Creole languages of the Caribbean Basin are essentially syntactically more alike than they are different in their underlying or deep structure, despite their surface phonological, morphological, and lexical differences.

6. Creole languages all adhere to linguistic standards. This means it is linguistically correct to speak of Standard English, as well as Standard Jamaican, Standard Haitian, Standard Sranan Tongo, etc., with these latter languages being separate languages and not dialects of English or Dutch.

7. These standards adhere to the rules of their own grammar, which makes communication reliable, uniform, and possible among speakers of the various Creole languages.

8. Creole is not the name of a language, but the family name of several distinct languages which include Jamaican, Haitian, Garifuna, Sranan Tongo — and, yes, Afrikaans (in South Africa) and Yiddish (in Israel and other countries around the world).

9. All human languages belong to language families: as examples English, German, Dutch, Danish, Swedish (to Germanic); Spanish, Italian, French, Portuguese (to Latinate or Romance); Chinese, Korean, Japanese (to Sino-Sinnitic), etc. Languages which belong to the same language families can be expected to share similar phonological, lexical,

morphological, and syntactic features; but they are different enough to be recognized as different languages, and not dialects of one another.

10. Languages, in general, are named after the countries that produced them natively: English(England); German (Germany); French(France); Spanish(Spain); Russian (Russia). Occasionally languages bear the name of ethnic or cultural affiliations. This logically suggests that the language of Jamaica should more properly be called "Jamaican" — certainly not "Patwa" or "Patois" which is a derisive term that was spawned by Europeans within a colonial imperialistic paradigm to describe and to maintain relations of inequity between 'slave' and 'master.' These terms should no longer be used, certainly not in Independent Jamaica.

11. All languages, including Jamaican, started out in spoken form only. That is a natural course of linguistic development. The written forms came afterwards. More importantly, all spoken languages can — without exception— be represented uniformly in writing.

12. When a language is represented uniformly in writing (i.e., when there is uniformity in phonemic-graphemic correspondence, prestige is given to the language around the world and literacy development of the speakers of that language is encouraged in the native language.

13. Most Jamaicans are bilingual to varying degrees in Jamaican and English. Of course, some Jamaicans are monolingual Jamaican, with a small percentage monolingual English (perhaps the British, Americans, or Canadians in Jamaica).

14. "Jamaican" is the native language of most of its speakers for whom English is indeed a second language.

15. It is psychologically uplifting and culturally empowering to be bilingual and biliterate!

GREEK-ENGLISH VOCABULARY[1]

A

ἀγαθός, -ή, -όν, *good*
ἀγαπάω, *I love*
ἀγάπη, -ης, ἡ, *love*
ἀγαπητός, -ή, όν, *beloved*
ἄγγελος, -ου, ὁ, *messenger, angel*
ἁγιάζω, *I sanctify*
ἅγιος, -α, -ον, *holy*
ἀγοράζω, *I buy*
ἄγω, *I lead, bring, go*; sec. aor., ἤγαγον.
ἀδελφός, -οῦ, ὁ, *brother*
ἄδικος, -ον, *unrighteous*
ἀδύνατος, -ον, *unable, impossible*
αἷμα, -ατος, τό, *blood*
αἴρω, *I take up, bear*
αἰσθάνομαι, *I perceive*
αἰτέω, *I ask for* (something)
αἰών, -ῶνος, ὁ, *age* (space of time), *world*
αἰώνιος, -α, -ον, *eternal*
ἀκάθαρτος, -ον, *unclean*
ἀκολουθέω, *I follow*
ἀκούω, *I hear*

---

1. Adapted from W.H. Davis, *Beginner's Grammar of the Greek New Testament* (Eugene, OR: Wipf & Stock), 225–270.

Greek-English Vocabulary

ἀκριβῶς, adv., *accurately*
ἀλέκτωρ, -ορος, ὁ, *cock*
ἀλήθεια, -ας, ἡ, *truth*
ἀληθής, -ές, *true*
ἀληθινός, -ή, -όν, *true*
ἀληθῶς, adv., *truly, surely*
ἀλλά, adversative conj., *but*
ἀλλήλων, (gen. masc. plu.), *of one another*
ἄλλος, -η, -ο, *other*
ἀλλότριος, -α, -ον, *belonging to another (another's), strange*
ἁμαρτάνω, *I sin*
ἁμαρτία, -ας, ἡ, *sin*
ἀμήν, adv., *truly, verily*
ἀμπελών, -ῶνος, ὁ, *vineyard*
ἀνά, prep., *on, upon, along*; only used with acc. in NT.
ἀναβαίνω, *I go up, come up, ascend*
ἀναβλέπω, *I look up, recover sight*
ἀναγινώσκω, *I read*
ἀνάστασις, -εως, ἡ, *resurrection*
ἄνεμος, -ου, ὁ, *wind*
ἀνήρ, ἀνδρός, ὁ, *man*
ἀνθίστημι, *I set against, withstand*
ἄνθρωπος, -ου, ὁ, *man*
ἀνίστημι, *I raise up, rise, arise*
ἀνοίγω, *I open*
ἀντί, prep., with gen., *opposite, against; instead of, in place of, for*
ἄνω, adv., *up, above*
ἄνωθεν, adv., *from above, again*
ἄξιος, -α, -ον, *fitting, worthy*
ἀπαγγέλλω, *I announce, declare*
ἀπαρνέομαι, *I deny*
ἅπας, ἅπασα, ἅπαν, *all, altogether*
ἀπέρχομαι, *I go away*
ἀπέχω, *I keep off, have in full* (of receipts); midd., *I keep myself from, abstain*
ἀπό, prep., *from off*, used only with the abl. in the N. T.

Greek-English Vocabulary

ἀποδίδωμι, *I give up, give back, restore; pay*; midd., *sell*
ἀποθνήσκω, *I die*
ἀποκρίνομαι, *I answer*
ἀποκτείνω, *I kill, slay*
ἀπολύω, *I release*
ἀποστέλλω, *I send forth*
ἀπόστολος, -ου, ὁ, *apostle*
ἅπτω, *I fasten to*; midd., ἅπτομαι, *I touch*
ἀρνέομαι, *I deny*
ἄρτι, adv., *now, just now, this moment*
ἄρτος, -ου, ὁ, *bread*
ἀρχή, -ῆς, ἡ *beginning*
ἀρχιερεύς, -έως, ὁ, *chief priest*
ἄρχομαι, *I begin*
ἄρχων, -οντος, ὁ, *ruler, prince*
ἀσθένεια, -ας, ἡ, *weakness*
ἀσθενής, -ές, *weak, sick*
αὔριον, adv., *tomorrow*
αὐτός, -ή, -ό, *self, very, same; he, she, it*
ἄφεσις, -εως, ἡ, *remission, forgiveness*
ἀφίημι, *I send away, forgive, leave, let*
ἀφίστημι, *I put away, depart from*
ἄφρων, -ον, *foolish*

B
βαίνω, *I go*
βάλλω, *I throw, cast*
βαπτίζω, *I baptize*
βασιλεία, -ας, ἡ, *kingdom*
βασιλεύς, -έως, ὁ, *king*
βασιλεύω, *I am king, I reign*
βιβλίον, -ου, τό, *book, a written document*
βίος, -ου, ὁ, *life, manner of life*
βλέπω, *I see, look at, behold*
βούλομαι, *I will, wish*

Greek-English Vocabulary

Γ

γάμος, -ου, ὁ, *marriage*
γάρ, coördinating conj., *for*.
γέ, enclitic, postpositive particle giving especial prominence to a word, *indeed, at last*
γεννάω, *I beget*
γένος, -ους, τό, *race, kind*
γῆ, γῆς, ἡ, *earth*
γίνομαι, *I become, be*
γινώσκω, *I know*
γλῶσσα, -ης, ἡ, *tongue*
γνῶσις, -εως, ἡ, *knowledge*
γόνυ, -νατος, τό, *knee*
γράμμα, -ατος, τό, *letter* (of alphabet), *writing*
γραμματεύς, -έως, ὁ, *scribe, town-clerk*
γραφή, -ῆς, ἡ, *writing, scripture*
γράφω, *I write*
γυνή, -ναικός, ἡ, *woman, wife*

Δ

δαιμόνιον, -ου, τό, *demon, evil-spirit*
δέ, copulative and adversative (milder than ἀλλά) conj., postpositive, *in the next place, and; but, on the other hand*
δεῖ, *it is necessary*
δεύτερος, -α, -ον, *second*
διά, prep., with gen., *through, by*; with acc., *because of, on account of, for the sake of*
διάβολος, -ου, ὁ, *devil*
διαθήκη, -ης, ἡ, *covenant, testament*
διακονέω, *I serve, minister*
διακονία, -ας, ἡ, *service, ministry*
διάκονος, -ου, ὁ, *servant, minister, deacon*
διαλογίζομαι, *I reason with, discuss, consider*
διάνοια, -ας, ἡ, *mind, understanding*
διδάσκαλος, -ου, ὁ, *teacher*
διδάσκω, *I teach*

Greek-English Vocabulary

δίδωμι, *I give, deliver*
διέρχομαι, *I go through*
δίκαιος, -α, -ον, *righteous*
δικαιοσύνη, -ης, ἡ, *righteousness*
δικαιόω, *I declare righteous, justify*
διψάω, *I thirst*
διώκω, *I follow after, pursue, persecute*
δοκέω, *I think, suppose;* δοκεῖ, *it seems good*
δόξα, -ης, ἡ, *glory*
δοξάζω, *I glorify*
δουλεύω, *I am a servant, I serve*
δοῦλος, -ου, ὁ, *servant*
δύναμαι, *I am able, can*
δύναμις, -εως, ἡ, *power*
δυνατός, -ή, -όν, *able*
δύο, *two*
δώδεκα, *twelve*
δῶρον, -ου, τό, *gift*

E

ἐάν, conditional particle, *if*
ἐὰν μή, with a substantive = *except, unless*
ἑαυτοῦ, -ῆς, -οῦ, (rarely αὐτοῦ, -ῆς, -οῦ), reflexive, *himself, herself, itself*
ἔβαλον, *I threw, cast*; sec. aor. of βάλλω.
ἔβην, *I went*; μι- aorist of βαίνω.
ἐγενόμην, *I became*; sec. aor. of γίνομαι.
ἔγνων, *I knew*; μι- aorist of γινώσκω.
ἐγράφην, sec. aor. passive of γράφω.
ἐγγύς, adv., *near*
ἐγείρω, *I raise up*
ἐγώ, *I*
ἔθνος, -ους, τό, *race, nation*
ἔθος, -ους, τό, *custom*
εἰ, conditional particle, *if*
εἰ μή, with a substantive = *except, unless*

Greek-English Vocabulary

εἶδον, *I saw*; sec. aor.; ὁράω used in present
εἰμί, *I am*
εἶπον, εἶπα, *I said*; sec. aor.; λέγω used in present
εἰρήνη, -ης, ἡ, *peace*
εἰς, prep., *into*, used only with the acc.
εἷς, μία, ἕν, *one*

εἰσάγω, *I bring in*
εἰσέρχομαι, *I enter*
ἐκ. (ἐξ), prep., *out, out of, from within*, used only with the abl.
ἐκβάλλω, *I throw out, cast out*
ἐκεῖ, adv., *there*
ἐκεῖνος, -η, -ο, demons. pron., *that (one)*
ἐκκλησία, -ας, ἡ, *assembly, church*
ἐκπορεύομαι, *I go out*
ἐκτείνω, *I stretch out*
ἔλαβον, *I took*; sec. aor. of λαμβάνω.
ἔλεος, -ους, τό, *pity, mercy*
ἐλεύθερος, -α, -ον, *free*
ἐλπίζω, *I hope*
ἐλπίς, -ίδος, ἡ, *hope*
ἔλιπον, *I left*; sec. aor. of λείπω.
ἐμαυτοῦ, -ῆς, reflexive pron., *myself*
ἐμβαίνω, *I go into, embark*
ἐμός, -ή, όν, poss. pron., *my, mine*
ἐν, prep., *in*; used only with the loc.
ἐντολή, -ῆς, ἡ, *commandment*
ἐνώπιον, prep. with gen., *before, in the presence of*
ἐξέρχομαι, *I go out*; sec. aor. ἐξῆλθον.
ἔξεστιν, *it is lawful, is possible*
ἐξίστημι, *I am amazed, am beside myself*
ἐξουσία, -ας, ἡ, *authority, power*
ἔξω, adv., *without, outside*; used with abl., *without, outside*
ἑορτή, -ῆς, ἡ, *feast*
ἐπαγγελία, -ας, ἡ, *promise*
ἐπαύριον, adv., *on the morrow*

Greek-English Vocabulary

ἐπερωτάω, *I question, ask* (a question)
ἐπιγινώσκω, *I recognise, discover*
ἐπιδίδωμι, *I give over*
ἐπιθυμία, -ας, ἡ, *desire*
ἐπιθυμέω, *I desire*
ἐπιμένω, *I remain, abide*
ἐπιτίθημι, *I lay upon, place upon*
ἐργασία, -ας, ἡ, *work, business*
ἔργον, -ου, τό, *work*
ἔρημος, -ου, ἡ, *wilderness, desert*
ἔρχομαι, *I go, come*
ἐρωτάω, *I ask* (question)
ἐσθίω, *I eat;* ἔφαγον, *I ate*
ἔσχατος, -η, -ον, *last*
ἔσχον, *I got;* sec. aor. of ἔχω.
ἕτερος, -α, -ον, *another*
ἔτος, -ους, τό, *year*
εὖ, adv., *well*
εὐαγγελίζομαι, *I proclaim glad tidings* (preach the gospel)
εὐθέως, adv., *straightway, at once*
εὑρίσκω, *I find*
εὗρον, *I found;* sec. aor. of εὑρίσκω.
ἔφαγον, *I ate;* sec. aor.; ἐσθίω used in present
Ἐφέσιος, -α, -ον, *Ephesian*
ἐφίστημι, *I stand upon* or *by, come upon*
ἔφυγον, sec. aor. of φεύγω.
ἔχω, *I have, hold, get*

Z
ζάω, *I live*
ζηλόω, *I am jealous, desire eagerly*
ζητέω, *I seek*
ζωή, -ῆς, ἡ, *life*

H
ἤ, conj., *or*

Greek-English Vocabulary

ἡγεμών, -όνος, ὁ, *leader, governor*
ᾔδειν, old pluperf. (with pres. meaning) of οἶδα.
ἦλθον, *I went, came*; sec. aor.; ἔρχομαι used in present
ἥλιος, -ου, ὁ, *sun*
ἡμέρα, -ας, ἡ, *day*
ἡμέτερος, -α, -ον, poss. pron., *our*

Θ

θάλασσα, -ης, ἡ, *sea*
θάνατος, -ου, ὁ, *death*
θανατόω, *I put to death*
θαυμάζω, *I wonder, marvel*
θεάομαι, *I behold, see, look at*
θέλημα, -ατος, τό, *will*
θέλω, *I wish, will*
θεός, -οῦ, ὁ, *God*
θεραπεύω, *I heal, doctor*
θεωρέω, *I look at, gaze, see*
θλίψις, -εως, ἡ, *tribulation, distress*
θρίξ, τριχός, ἡ, *hair*
θρόνος, -ου, ὁ, *throne*
θυγάτηρ, -τρός, ἡ, *daughter*

Ι

ἰάομαι, *I heal*
ἴδιος, -α, -ον, *one's own*
ἱερόν, -οῦ, τό, *temple*
ἱερεύς, -έως, ὁ, *priest*
ἵημι, *I send*
ἵνα, conj. generally with subjunctive, *in order that, that*
ἱμάτιον, -ου, τό, *garment*
ἵστημι, *I make to stand, place, stand*
ἰσχυρός, -ά, -όν, *strong*

Κ

καθαρίζω, *I purify*

Greek-English Vocabulary

καθίστημι, *I set down, appoint*
καί, conj., *and; also; even;* καὶ ... καὶ, *both ... and*
κακός, -ή, -όν, *evil, bad*
καλέω, *I call*
καλός, -ή, -όν, *good, beautiful*
καλῶς, adv., *well, finely*
καρδία, -ας, ἡ, *heart*
καρπός, -οῦ, ὁ, *fruit*
κατά, prep., with gen., *down (upon), against;* with abl., *down (from);* with acc., *down (along), through, according to*
κατβαίνω, *I am going down*
καταλύω, *I destroy*
κατεσθίω, *I eat up*
κεῖμαι, *I lie (am laid)*
κεφαλή, -ῆς, ἡ, *head*
κηρύσσω, *I announce, proclaim*
κοινός, ή όν, *common, unclean*
κοινόω, *I make common, unclean*
κόπτω, *I beat, strike*
κόσμος, -ου, ὁ, *world*
κράβαττος, -ου, ὁ, *pallet, bed*
κράζω, *I cry out*
κρίμα, -ατός, τό, *judgment*
κρίνω, *I judge*
κρίσις -εως, ἡ, *judgement*
κρύπτω, *I hide*
κτίσις, -εως, ἡ, *creation*
κυριεύω, *I am lord of, rule (over)* with gen.
κύριος, -ου, ὁ, *Lord*
κύων, κυνός, ὁ, *dog*
κωλύω, *I hinder*
κώμη, -ης, ἡ, *village*

Λ
λαλέω, *I speak*
λαμβάνω, *I take, receive;* sec. aor., ἔλαβον.

λαός, -οῦ, ὁ, *people*
λέγω, *I say, speak*
λείπω, *I leave, abandon*; sec. aor., ἔλιπον.
λῃστής, -οῦ, ὁ, *robber*
λίθος, -ου, ὁ, *stone*
λίψ, λιβός. ὁ, *the S. W. wind*
λόγος, -ου, ὁ, *word*
λούω, *I wash*
λυπέω, *I grieve*
λύω, *I loose*

M

μαθητής, -οῦ, ὁ, *disciple*
μακάριος, -α, -ον, *happy, blessed*
μᾶλλον, adv., *more, rather*
μανθάνω, *I learn*; sec. aor., ἔμαθον.
μαρτυρέω, *I bear witness testify*
μάστιξ, -ιγος, ἡ, *whip, scourge, plague*
μάχαιρα, -ας, ἡ, *sword*
μέγας, μεγάλη, μέγα, *great*
μέλει, *it concerns, is a care,* with dat.
μέλλω, *I am about* (or *going*) *to do* something
μέλος, -ους, τό, *member*
μένω, *I remain*
μέρος,-ους, τό, *part*
μετά, prep., with gen., *with*; with acc., *after*; μετὰ ταῦτα, *after these things, after this*
μεταβαίνω, *I pass over, depart*
μετανοέω, *I repent*
μή, *not*
μηδείς, μηδεμία, μηδέν, *no one, nothing*
μήτε . . . μήτε, *neither . . . nor*
μήτηρ, -τρός, ἡ, *mother*
μικρός, -ά, -όν, *small, little*
μισέω, *I hate*
μισθός, -οῦ, ὁ, *pay, wages, reward*

Greek-English Vocabulary

μνᾶ, μνᾶς, ἡ, mina (a weight and a sum of money)
μνημεῖον, -ου, τό, sepulchre, tomb
μνημονεύω, I remember, with gen.
μονογενής, -ές, only begotten
μόνον, adv., only
μόνος, -η, -ον, only, alone
μυστήριον, -ου, τό, mystery

N

ναός, -οῦ, ὁ, temple
νεανίας, -ου, ὁ, youth
νεκρός, -ά, -όν, dead
νέος, -α, -ον, young, new
νεφέλη, -ης, ἡ, cloud
νεωκόρος, -ου, ὁ or ἡ, temple-keeper
νηστεύω, I fast
νικάω, I conquer
νίπτω, I wash
νομίζω, I think, suppose
νόμος, -ου, ὁ, law
νῦν, adv., now
νύξ, νυκτός, ἡ, night

O

ὁ, ἡ, τό, the definite article the
ὁδός, -οῦ, ἡ, way, road
οἶδα, I know
οἰκία, -ας, ἡ, house
οἰκοδομέω, I build
οἶκος, -ου, ὁ, house
οἶνος, -ου, ὁ, wine
ὀλίγος, -η, -ον, few, little, small
ὅλος, -η, -ον, whole
ὁμοιόω, I make like
ὁμολογέω, I agree with, confess
ὄνομα, -ατος, τό, name

Greek-English Vocabulary

ὅπου, rel. adv., *where*
ὅπτομαι, *I see*
ὁράω, *I see*; fut., ὄψομαι; sec. aor., εἶδον
ὅς, ἥ, ὅ, rel. pron., *who, which, that, what*
ὅστις, ἥτις, ὅτι, indef. rel. pron., *who, which, that, what*
ὅταν, rel. temporal adv. used with the subj. and ind., *whenever, when*
ὅτε, rel. temporal adv. used with the ind., *when*
ὅτι, conj., *because, that*
οὐ, *not*; οὐκ before vowels; οὐχ before rough breathing
οὐ μή, double negative, *no way! Definitely not*
οὐδείς, οὐδεμία, οὐδέν, *no one (nobody), nothing*
οὐκέτι, *no longer, no more*
οὐρανός, -οῦ, ὁ, *heaven*
οὖς, ὠτός, τό, *ear*
οὔτε . . . οὔτε, *neither . . . nor*
οὗτος, αὕτη, τοῦτο, demons. pron., *this (one)*
ὀφείλω, *I owe, ought*; sec. aor. without augment, ὄφελον
ὀφθαλμός, -οῦ, ὁ, *eye*
ὄχλος, -ου, ὁ, *crowd*
ὄψομαι, fut. midd., *I shall see*; ὁράω used in present

Π

παιδίον, -ου, τό, *little child*
παλαιός, -ά, -όν, *old, ancient*
πάλιν, adv., *again*
παρά, prep., with the loc., *by* or *at (the side of)*; with the abl., *from (the side of)*; with the acc., *along (side of)*
παραβολή, -ῆς, ἡ, *parable*
παραδίδωμι, *I give over (to another), deliver up, betray*
παρακαλέω, *I beseech, exhort, encourage*
παράκλησις, -εως, ἡ, *exhortation*
παραλαμβάνω, *I take, receive*; sec. aor., παρέλαβον
παρατίθημι, *I set before, commit*
παρέχω, *I provide, supply*
παρίστημι, *I place beside, stand by*

Greek-English Vocabulary

παρουσία -ας, ἡ, *coming, presence*
πᾶς, πᾶσα, πᾶν, *all, every*
πάσχα, (indeclinable), τό, *the Passover*
πάσχω, *I suffer*; sec. aor., ἔπαθον
πατήρ, -τρός, ὁ, *father*
παύω, *I stop*; midd., παύομαι, *I cease*
πείθω, *I persuade*
πεινάω, *I hunger, am hungry*
πειράζω, *I test, tempt*
πέμπω, *I send*
περί, prep., with gen., *about, concerning*; with abl., *from around*; with acc., *round about, about, concerning*
περιάγω, *I go about, carry about*
περιπατέω, *I walk, live*
περισσός, -ή, -όν, *abundant*
πιστεύω, *I believe*
πίστις, -εως, ἡ, *faith*
πιστός, -ή, -όν, *faithful*
πλανάω, *I cause to wander* (to err), *lead astray*
πλῆθος, -ους, τό, *crowd, multitude*
πληρόω, *I make full, fill*
πλησίον, adv., *near*; ὁ πλησίον, *neighbor*
πλοῖον, -ου, τό, *boat*
πλούσιος, -α, -ον, *rich*
πνεῦμα, -ατος, τό, *spirit*
πόθεν, interrog. adv., *whence*
ποιέω, *I do, make*
ποιμήν, -ένος, ὁ, *shepherd*
πόλις, -εως, ἡ, *city*
πολύ, adv., *much*
πολύς, πολλή, πολύ, *much, many*
πονηρός, -ά, -όν, *evil*
πορεύομαι, *I go, proceed*
ποτήριον, -ου, τό, *cup*
ποῦ, interrog. adv., *where*
πούς, ποδός, ὁ, *foot*

Greek-English Vocabulary

πρεσβύτερος, -ου, ὁ, *elder*
πρίν (ἤ), *before*;
πρό, prep. with abl., *before*
προάγω, *I lead forth, go before*
πρόβατον, -ου, τό, *sheep*
πρός, prep., with loc., *near, by*; with acc., *towards, to*; with abl. (once), *"from the point of view of"*
προσέρχομαι, *I go to, come to*
προσευχή, -ῆς, ἡ, *prayer*
προστίθημι, *I add, give in addition*
πρόσωπον, -ου, τό, *face*
προφητεύω, *I prophesy*
προφήτης, -ου, ὁ, *prophet*
πρῶτος, -η, -ον, *first*
πώποτε, adv., *ever yet*
πῶς, adv., *how*

Ρ
ῥῆμα, -ατος, τό, *word*

Σ
σάββατον, -ου, τό, *Sabbath*
σαλεύω, *I shake*
σάλπιγξ, -ιγγος, ἡ, *trumpet*
σάρξ, σαρκός, ἡ, *flesh*
σεαυτοῦ, -ῆς, reflexive, *thyself*
σημεῖον, -ου, τό, *sign*
σήμερον, adv., *to-day, this day*
σιγάω, *I am silent, keep silence*
σιωπάω, *I am silent, keep silence*
σκανδαλίζω, *I cause to stumble, offend*
σκηνόω, *I dwell* (as in a tent)
σκόλοψ, -οπος, ὁ *stake, thorn*
σκοτία, -ας, ἡ, *darkness*
σκότος, -ους, τό, *darkness*
σός, σή, σόν, poss. pron., *thy, thine*

σοφία, -ας, ἡ, *wisdom*
σοφός, -ή, -όν, *wise*
σπείρω, *I sow*
σπέρμα, -ατος, τό, *seed*
σταυρός, -οῦ, ὁ, *cross*
σταυρόω, *I crucify*
στέλλω, *I send*
στενάζω, *I groan*
στόμα, -ατος, τό, *mouth*
στρέφω, *I turn, change*
σύ, *thou (you)*
σύν, prep., *with*, used only with the instrumental
συνάγω, *I gather together*
συναγωγή, -ῆς, ἡ, *synagogue*
συνεσθίω, *I eat with* (someone)
συνίημι, *I perceive*
συνίστημι, *I commend, establish*
σύρω, *I drag, draw*
σώζω, *I save*
σῶμα, -ατος, τό, *body*
σωτήρ, -ῆρος, ὁ, *Saviour*
σωτηρία, -ας, ἡ, *salvation*
σώφρων, -ον, *of sound mind, sober-minded*

Τ
ταπεινόω, *I make low, humble*
ταχέως, adv., *quickly*
ταχύ, adv., *quickly*
τὲ ... καὶ, *both ... and*
τέκνον, -ου, τό, *child*
τέλειος, -α, -ον, *finished, complete*
τελειόω, *I end, complete, fulfill*
τελευτάω, (*I finish*), *I die*
τελέω, *I finish, end, complete*
τέλος, -ους, τό, *end*
τέσσαρες, τέσσαρα, *four*

Greek-English Vocabulary

τέταρτος, -η, -ον, *fourth*
τηρέω, *I keep*
τίθημι, *I place, lay, put down*
τιμάω, *I honor*
τίς, τί, interrog. pron., *who, which, what*
τις, τι, indef. pron., *one, a certain one, a certain thing; some one, something*
τολμάω, *I dare*
τόπος, -ου, ὁ, *place*
τότε, adv., *then*
τοῦτο, see οὗτος
τρεῖς, τρία, *three*
τρίτος, -η, -ον, *third*
τυφλός, -ή, -όν, *blind*
τυφλόω, *I make blind, blind*
ὑγιής, -ές, *whole, healthy*
ὕδωρ, ὕδατος, τό, *water*
υἱός, -οῦ, ὁ, *son*
ὑμέτερος, -α, -ον, poss. pron., *your*
ὑπάγω, *I go away, depart*
ὑπέρ, prep., with abl., *in behalf of, in the interest of; instead of; in place of; for the sake of; about, concerning;* with acc., *over, above, beyond*
ὑπό, prep., with abl., *by;* with acc., *under*
ὑποκριτής, -οῦ, ὁ, *pretender, hypocrite*

Φ

φαίνω, *I shine, appear*
φανερός, -ά, -όν, *manifest*
φανερόω, *I make manifest*
φέρω, *I bear, carry*
φεύγω, *I flee, take flight;* sec. aor., ἔφυγον
φιλέω, *I love*
φίλος, -ου, ὁ, *friend*
φοβέομαι, *I am afraid, I fear*
φόβος, -ου, ὁ, *fear*

φυλάσσω, *I guard, keep*
φωνέω, *I call, speak aloud*
φωνή, -ῆς, ἡ, *voice*
φῶς, φωτός, τό, *light*

Χ
χαίρω, *I rejoice*
χαρά, -ᾶς, ἡ, *joy*
χάρις, -ιτος, ἡ, *grace*
χάρισμα, -ατος, τό, *gift, free gift*
χείρ, χειρός, ἡ, *hand*
χρεία, -ας, ἡ, *need*
χρονίζω, *I spend time, tarry*
χρόνος, -ου, ὁ, *time*

Ψ
ψεύστης, -ου, ὁ, *liar*
ψυχή, -ῆς, ἡ, *soul*

Ω
ὧδε, adv., *here, hither*
ὥρα, -ας, ἡ, *hour*
ὡς, rel., comp., and temporal adv., *as, when*
ὥστε, consecutive particle, *so that*
ὥστε, inferential conj., *and so, therefore*

HELPFUL MATERIAL

Abbot-Smith, G. *A Manual Greek Lexicon of the New Testament*. Edinburgh: T & T Clark, 1937.
Adams, L. Emilie. *Understanding Jamaican Patois: An Introduction to Afro-Jamaican Grammar* Kingston: LMH Publishers 1991.
Aland, Kurt, et al., eds. *The Greek New Testament*. New York: United Bible Societies, 1983.
Allsopp, Richard. *Dictionary of Caribbean English Usage*. Oxford: Oxford University Press, 1996.
Barr, James. *The Semantics of Biblical Language*. Oxford: Oxford University Press, 1961.
Bauer, W., W. F. Arndt, F. W. Gingrich and F. W. Danker, eds. *A Greek-English Lexicon of the New Testament and Other Early Christian Literature*. Chicago: Chicago University Press, 2000.
Black, David Alan. *Linguistics and New Testament Interpretation: Essays on Discourse Analysis*. Nashville: Broadman Press, 1984.
Blass, F., A. Debrunner, and R. Funk. *A Greek Grammar of the New Testament and Other Early Christian Literature*. Chicago: University Press, 1961.
Boyer, J. L. "Second-Class Conditions in New Testament Greek." *Grace Theological Journal* 3 (1982): 81–88.
Bullinger, E. W. 1968 *Figures of Speech Used in the Bible Explained and Illustrated*. Grand Rapids: Eerdmans.
Campbell, E. Christine. "Language and Identity in Caribbean Theology," in *A Karios Moment in Caribbean Theology*, edited by G. Lincoln Roper and J. Richard Middleton. Eugene, OR: Pickwick, 2013.
Carson, D.A. *Greek Accents: A Students Guide*. Grand Rapids: Baker, 1995.
Christie, Pauline. *Language in Jamaica*. Kingston: Arawak Publications, 2003.
Cotterell, Peter. *Language and the Christian: A Guide to Communication and Understanding* London: Samuel Bagster & Sons, 1978.
———, and Max Turner, *Linguistics and Biblical Interpretation*. Downers Grove, Illinois: InterVarsity Press, 1989).

Helpful Material

Dana, H. E. and J. R. Mantey *Manual Grammar of the Greek New Testament.* Toronto: Macmillan, 1955.

Davis, W.H. *Beginner's Grammar of the Greek New Testament.* Eugene, OR: Wipf & Stock, 2005.

Deissmann, G. Adolph. *Light from the Ancient East.* London: Hodder and Stoughton, 1910.

Dennis, Carlton. *Elements of Greek.* Kingston, JA: SRI, 2013.

Earle, Ralph. *Word Meanings in the New Testament.* Grand Rapids: Baker, 1982.

Fee, Gordon D. *New Testament Exegesis: A Handbook for Students and Pastors.* Louisville: Westminster, 1993;

Gayle, Bertram et al. *Di Jamiekan Nyuu Testiment* Kingston: Bible Society of the West Indies, 2012.

Guthrie George H. and J. Scott Duvall, *Biblical Greek Exegesis, A Graded Approach to Learning Intermediate and Advanced Greek* . Grand Rapids: Zondervan, 1998.

Holmes, Michael, ed. *The Greek New Testament.* Atlanta: SBL, 2010. http://sblgnt.com/.

Louw, Johannes P., "Discourse Analysis and the Greek New Testament," *The Bible Translator* 24 (1973): 108–118.

———, and Eugene A. Nida, eds. *Greek-English Lexicon of the New Testament Based on Semantic Domains.* New York: United Bible Societies, 1988.

Metzger, Bruce M. *A Textual Commentary on the Greek New Testament.* Stuttgart: Deutsche Bibelgesellschaft, 1994.

Metzger, Bruce M.. *The Bible in Translation: Ancient and English Versions.* Grand Rapids: Baker, 2001.

Moulton, J. H. and George Milligan. *The Vocabulary of the Greek Testament.* Grand Rapids: Eerdmans, 1930.

Mounce, William D. *A Graded Reader of Biblical Greek* (Grand Rapids: Zondervan, 1996);

Muir, Susan. "Linguistics for Students of Koine Greek." In *Greek 2000: Elemental Overview/Exegetical Preview.* Kingston: Jahmeckyah, 2000.

Murrell, Nathaniel Samuel. "Hermeneutics as Interpretation and the Caribbean Student." *Binah* 2 (1997):7–28.

Nida, E. A. "Paradoxes of Translation." *The Bible Translator* 42 (1991):5–26.

Phillips, J. B. *Ring of Truth: A Translator's Testimony.* London: Hodder and Stoughton, 1967.

Porter, Stanley et. al., *Fundamentals of NT Greek.* Grand Rapids: Eerdmans, 2010.

Porter, S., and D. A. Carson (eds.). *Biblical Greek Language and Linguistics: Open Questions in Current Research.* Sheffield: Sheffield Academic Press, 1993.

Rienecker, Fritz. *Linguistic Key to the Greek New Testament.* Grand Rapids: Zondervan, 1980.

Robertson, A. T. and W. Hersey Davis. *A New Short Grammar of the Greek New Testament.* Grand Rapids: Baker, 1977.

Helpful Material

Silva, Moises. *Biblical Words and Their Meaning: An Introduction to Lexical Semantics*. Grand Rapids: Academic Books, 1983.
Wallace, Daniel B. *Greek Grammar Beyond the Basics*. Grand Rapids: Zondervan, 1996.
Writing Jamaican the Jamaican Way/Ou fi Rait Jamiekan. The Jamaican Language Unit/Di Jamiekan Langwij Yuunit: Kingston: Arawak, 2009.
Yorke, Gosnell. "Bible Translation in Anglophone Africa and Her Diaspora: A Postcolonialist Agenda." *Black Theology: An International Journal* 2: (2004) 153–166.
Young, Richard A. *Intermediate New Testament Greek: A Linguistic and Exegetical Approach*. Nashville: Broadman & Holman, 1994.
Zerwick, M., and M. Grosvenor. *A Grammatical Analysis of the Greek New Testament*. Rome: PBI, 1979.

www.ingramcontent.com/pod-product-compliance
Lightning Source LLC
Chambersburg PA
CBHW070447090426
42735CB00012B/2479